Creating the Ultimate Soccer Player:

Realize the Secrets and Tricks Used by the Best Professional Soccer Players and Coaches to Improve Your Athleticism, Conditioning, Nutrition, and Mental Toughness

By
Joseph Correa
Professional Athlete and Coach

COPYRIGHT

ACKNOWLEDGEMENTS

To my family, for their unconditional love and support during the creation of and development of this book.

Creating the Ultimate Soccer Player:

Realize the Secrets and Tricks Used by the Best Professional Soccer Players and Coaches to Improve Your Athleticism, Conditioning, Nutrition, and Mental Toughness

By
Joseph Correa
Professional Athlete and Coach

ABOUT THE AUTHOR

Having performed as a professional athlete, I understand what goes through your mind and how difficult it can be to improve your performance and take it to the next level.

The three biggest changes in my life have come from improving my strength and conditioning, enhanced flexibility, and **increased ability to focus through meditation and visualization**. Meditation and visualization have helped me control my emotions and simulate live competitions before they even happened.

Adding yoga and extended periods of stretching have reduced my injuries to almost zero and have improved my reaction and speed.

Improving my nutrition has more than allowed me to continue performing at my peak under difficult climatic conditions which might have affected me in the past causing cramps and muscle pulls.

By far, meditation and visualization will change everything no matter what athletic discipline you're in. You will see how powerful it is once you spend more and more time on it and dedicate a minimum of 10 minutes a day to breathing, focused thinking, and concentrating.

INTRODUCTION

To reach your true potential you need to be at your optimal physical and mental condition and in order to do this you need to start an organized plan that will help you develop your strength, mobility, nutrition, and mental toughness. This book will do that. Eating right and training hard are two of the pieces of the puzzle but you need the third piece to make it all happen. The third piece is mental toughness and that can be obtained through meditation and visualization techniques taught in this book.

This book will provide you with the following:

-Normal and advanced training calendars
-Dynamic warm-up exercises
-High performance training exercises
-Active recovery exercises
-Nutrition calendar to increase muscle
-Nutrition calendar to burn fat
-Muscle building recipes
-Fat burning recipes
-Advanced breathing techniques to enhance performance
-Meditation techniques
-Visualization techniques
-Visualization sessions to improve performance

Physical conditioning and strength training, smart nutrition, and advanced meditation/visualization techniques are the three keys to achieve optimal performance. Most athletes are missing one or two of these fundamental ingredients but by making the decision to change you will have the potential to achieve a new "ULTIMATE" you.

Athletes who begin this training plan will see the following:

- Increased muscle growth
- Reduced stress levels
- Enhanced strength, mobility, and reaction
- Better capacity to focus for long periods of time
- Become faster and more enduring
- Lower muscle fatigue
- Faster recovery times after competing or training
- Increased flexibility
- Overcome nervousness better
- Better control over you breathing
- Control over your emotions under pressure

Make the choice. Make the change. Make a new "ULTIMATE" you.

CONTENTS

CHAPTER 1: HIGH PERFORMANCE TRAINING EXERCISES FOR SOCCER

HIGH PERFORMANCE CALENDAR "NORMAL"

NORMAL

Sunday	Monday	Tuesday	Wednesday	Thursday	Friday	Saturday
				1	2	3
4	5 Upper body split Gamma	6 Active recovery Gamma	7 Lower body split Gamma	8 Core split Gamma	9 Active recovery Gamma	10 Speed/ Explosive Split
11 Active recovery	12 Upper body split Delta	13 Active recovery Delta	14 Lower body split Delta	15 Core split Delta	16 Active recovery Delta	17 Speed/ Explosive Split
18 Active recovery	19 Upper body split Gamma	20 Active recovery Gamma	21 Lower body split Gamma	22 Core split Gamma	23 Active recovery Gamma	24 Speed/ Explosive Split
25 Active recovery	26 Upper body split Delta	27 Active recovery Delta	28 Lower body split Delta	29 Core split Delta	30 Active recovery Delta	31 Speed/ Explosive Split

INSTRUCTIONS:

FOUR PER WEEK

Each week you will complete 4 different workouts that target different areas of the body. This is to ensure that your body is constantly forced to adapt.

CUSTOMIZE YOUR EXERCISES

Each split (upper, lower, core and speed/explosiveness) will have 10 different exercises that you can choose from.

PREMADE TEMPLATE

You can also choose to follow our pre-made calendar to ensure that you improve all aspects of your athleticism.

HIGH PERFORMANCE CALENDAR "ADVANCED"

ADVANCED

Sunday	Monday	Tuesday	Wednesday	Thursday	Friday	Saturday
				1	2	3
4	5 Upper body split Gamma	6 Active recovery Gamma	7 Lower body split Gamma	8 Core split Gamma	9 Active recovery Gamma	10 Speed/ Explosive Split
11 Active recovery	12 Upper body split Delta	13 Active recovery Delta	14 Lower body split Delta	15 Core split Delta	16 Active recovery Delta	17 Speed/ Explosive Split
18 Active recovery	19 Upper body split Gamma	20 Active recovery Gamma	21 Lower body split Gamma	22 Core split Gamma	23 Active recovery Gamma	24 Speed/ Explosive Split
25 Active recovery	26 Upper body split Delta	27 Active recovery Delta	28 Lower body split Delta	29 Core split Delta	30 Active recovery Delta	31 Speed/ Explosive Split

INSTRUCTIONS:

FOUR PER WEEK

Each week you will complete 4 different workouts that target different areas of the body. This is to ensure that your body is constantly forced to adapt.

CUSTOMIZE YOUR EXERCISES

Each split (upper, lower, core and speed/explosiveness) will have 10 different exercises that you can choose from.

PREMADE TEMPLATE

You can also choose to follow our pre-made calendar to ensure that you improve all aspects of your athleticism.

HOW DO I READ THE CALENDAR?

The first calendar is your normal level athlete and is described as "NORMAL". This is what you should follow under normal circumstances.

The second calendar is the plus version and is described as "ADVANCED". This is what you should follow should you choose to increase the intensity. For this version, double the sets that are assigned but not the rep range.

WHAT WILL I BE ABLE TO ACCOMPLISH AFTER THIS PROGRAM?

The purpose of the workout is to improve all aspects of physical performance: strength, agility, power and endurance. As such, it is the perfect complement to a healthy diet for any athlete.

DYNAMIC WARM-UP EXERCISES

These are a set of 4 exercises (outside of the 40 main exercises) that the athlete will have to complete before each workout (referred to as split in this book). On active recovery days, the athlete will be expected to complete these exercises in combination with a 30 minute session of moderate cardio instead of 15.

a. **Roll-over's into V-sits:** Start by sitting down on the floor. Next propel yourself backwards by rolling your knees inward so that they touch your chest (your weight should be on the back now) with your arms extended on the ground. Finally, roll back to forward position and spread your legs so that they form a V shape. Perform 15 times.

b. **Fire Hydrants:** Start by getting down on your knees, palms flat on the ground (shoulder width). Ensure that your back is straight. Without moving your back, draw a circle with your knee so that it moves outward, forward and back. Repeat for each leg 15 times.

c. **Squat and hold:** Perform a squat and hold when at the bottom position for 30 seconds.

d. Forward lunges: Perform lunges by moving forward each time. 12 reps each leg (24 reps total).

HIGH PERFORMANCE TRAINING EXERCISES

Upper-Body Exercises

These are the exercises that you will complete on the days marked "Upper body split" in your calendar.

1. Negative push-ups (chest)

How to:
a. Lie down on the floor facedown and position your hands at shoulder width apart.
b. Slowly lower yourself downward until chest is fist length from the floor (tempo: 3 seconds).
c. Rapidly push yourself upward (Tempo: 1 second).

Rep scheme:

***3 sets of 12 repetitions. Each set should be difficult but you should not reach complete failure. You should be able to do 2-3 more reps after the 12th rep. Adjust repetition range until criteria is met but do not change the number of sets.

Health benefits:

+++Strength, ++ Flexibility, ++ Strengthening of joints

2. Diamond push-ups (triceps, chest)

How to:

a. Lie down on the floor facedown and position your hands narrower than shoulder width apart.
b. Slowly lower yourself downward until chest is a fist length from the floor
c. Push yourself upward

Rep scheme:

***3 sets of 12 repetitions. Each set should be difficult but you should not reach complete failure. You should be able to do 2-3 more reps after the 12th rep. Adjust repetition range until criteria is met but do not change the number of sets.

Health benefits:

+++Strength, +++ Endurance

3. **One arm push-ups (triceps, chest)**

How to:
a. Lie down on the floor facedown and position your hands shoulder width apart
b. Leave one arm in front of you and put the other on your back
c. Lower yourself downward and push yourself back up

Rep scheme:

***5 sets of 5 reps. if too difficult start at lower rep range and work yourself up. If still too difficult perform the exercises with your hands on an elevated platform (box, books etc.).

Health benefits:

+++Strength, +++Flexibility, +++Explosiveness

4. Pull-up (back, biceps)

How to:
a. Grab the bar shoulder width apart with palms facing forwards.
b. As you are hanging, slightly bring your torso back to form a small incline
c. Pull your torso up until the bar touches or is close to touching the upper portion of your chest
d. Lower yourself and repeat

Rep Scheme:

***3 sets of 10 reps. each set should be difficult but you should not reach complete failure. You should be able to do 2-3 more reps after the 10th rep. Adjust repetition range until criteria is met but do not change the number of sets.

Health benefits:

+++Strength, +++Endurance

5. Muscle up(chest, triceps, back)

How to:
a. Hang from a bar with thumbs on top of the bar (not around the bar)
b. Pull yourself up as if doing a pull-up
c. Roll your chest over the bar to transition from a pull-up position to a dip position
d. Lower yourself back down and repeat

Rep scheme: ***5 sets of 5 reps. if too difficult start at lower rep range and work yourself up. If still too difficult perform 10 sets of 1 rep to work your way up.

Health benefits:

+++Strength, ++Agility

6. Dips (triceps, chest)

How to:

a. Position your hands on each side of the bar so that your arms are fully extended and supporting yourself
b. Lower your body by bending at the elbow while ensuring that the movement is controlled
c. Press your body back up to starting position

Rep scheme:

***3 sets of 15 reps. each set should be difficult but you should not reach complete failure. You should be able to do 2-3 more reps after the 15th rep. Adjust repetition range until criteria is met but do not change the number of sets.

7. L-shaped pull-up (back, biceps)

How to:

a. Position yourself in a regular pull-up position
b. Lift your legs up as if to perform a leg raise (legs should form a 90-degree angle with your torso)
c. Pull yourself up as much as possible just like a regular pull-up
d. Lower yourself and repeat

Rep scheme:

***5 sets of 5 reps. if too difficult, lower the reps but not the sets until you can perform all 5 sets.

Health benefits:

++++ Strength, +++Flexibility, ++Endurance

8. Wide-grip pull-up(back)

How to:
a. Grab the bar wider than shoulder width apart with palms facing forwards.
b. As you are hanging, slightly bring your torso back to form a small incline
c. Pull your torso up until the bar touches or is close to touching the upper portion of your chest
d. Lower yourself and repeat

Rep Scheme:

***3 sets of 10 reps. each set should be difficult but you should not reach complete failure. You should be able to do 2-3 more reps after the 10th rep. Adjust repetition range until criteria is met but do not change the number of sets.

Health benefits:

+++Strength, +++Endurance

Delta X workout: perform exercises 1,3,5,8
Gamma workout: perform exercises 2,4,6,7

Lower-Body Exercises

These are the exercises that you will complete on the days marked "Lower body split" in your calendar.

1. Tuck Jump (glutes, quads)

How to:
a. Stand shoulder width apart with knees slightly bent
b. Jump, and bring in knees toward the chest and extend arms straight-up

Rep Scheme:

***3 sets of 20 repetitions.

Health benefits:

+++Explosive strength gains, ++Increased flexibility

2. Wall sit (glutes, quads)

How to:
a. Position back on a wall (facing the other side)
b. Squat/slide down until your thighs are parallel to the ground
c. Hold position

Rep Scheme:

***3 sets of 120 seconds.

Health benefits:

++Endurance, +++Lactic threshold, ++Strength

3. Lunge (quads)

How to:
a. Stand shoulder width apart
b. Step right leg forward as much as possible without overdoing it
c. Bend left leg until left knee is close to touching the floor
d. Stand back up
e. Repeat with left leg (bending the right)

Rep Scheme:

***3 sets of 15 reps.

Health benefits:

++Strength, ++Stability

4. Air Squat (glutes, quads)

How to:
a. Stand with your feet shoulder width apart
b. Sit down by moving your hips back
c. Ensure that you look up & forward as you perform the squat and your back is straight
d. Stand back up with legs fully extended

Rep Scheme:

***3 sets of 30 reps.

Health benefits:

+++Strength, ++Endurance

5. Close-stance squat (quads)

How to:

a. Stand with your feet as close together as possible without touching
b. Sit down by moving your hips back with your arms extended in front of you
c. Ensure that you look up& forward as you perform the squat and your back is straight
d. Stand back up with legs fully extended

Rep scheme:

***3 sets of 30 reps.

Health benefits:

+++Strength, ++Endurance, ++Balance

6. Drinking bird (hamstrings, quads)

How to:

a. Stand on one leg with a slight bend while positioning the other leg behind you
b. Bend forward so that the leg behind you is parallel with your back
c. Do this while fully extending your arms in front of you
d. Return to starting position and repeat

Rep scheme:

***10 reps per leg. One set.

Health benefits:

+++Balance, ++Endurance

7. Elevated single-leg calf raise (calves)

How to:

a. Stand on a ledge shoulder width apart so that your weight is on the front ball of your foot
b. Leave one leg on the ledge while placing the other slightly behind so that all your weight is on the ball of one foot
c. Lower yourself so as to contract the calf muscle

Rep scheme:

***2 sets of 20 reps per leg.

Health benefits:

+++Strength, ++Balance, ++Endurance

8. Hip thrusts (glutes)

How to:
a. Lie one the ground facing up
b. Bend your knees at a 90-degree angle
c. Lift your but off the ground with the help of your hands on each side
d. Lower and repeat

Rep scheme:

***3 sets of 12 reps. each set should be difficult but you should not reach complete failure. You should be able to do 2-3 more reps after the 12th rep. Adjust repetition range until criteria is met but do not change the number of sets.\

Health benefits:

+++Strength, ++Endurance

Delta X workout: perform exercises 1,3,5,8
Gamma workout: perform exercises 2,4,6,7

Core Exercises

These are the exercises that you will complete on the days marked "Core split" in your calendar.

1. Plank

How to:
a. Lie down the floor facedown and position your arms shoulder width apart
b. Ensure that you support your weight with your toes and forearms
c. Hold position

Rep Scheme:

***3 sets of 120 seconds.

Health benefits:

++Endurance, +++Lactic threshold, +++Core stability

2. Russian twist

How to:
a. Lie down on the floor (sit)with legs bent at the knees
b. Make sure your torso is upright so that it makes a V with your thighs
c. Extend your arms (with or without holding a weight) and twist your torso to the right as much as you can
d. Repeat by twisting to your left

Rep Scheme:

***3 sets of 20 reps. each set should be difficult but you should not reach complete failure. You should be able to do 2-3 more reps after the 20th rep. Adjust repetition range until criteria is met but do not change the number of sets.

Health benefits:

++Strength, +++Core stability

3. Leg raise

How to:
a. Lie down on the floor with your legs straight
b. Place your hands next to your glutes on each side
c. Lift your legs up to make a 90-degree angle while ensuring that your legs aren't bending (your hands should help you balance yourself and be pushing on the floor)

Rep Scheme:

***3 sets of 20 reps. each set should be difficult but you should not reach complete failure. You should be able to do 2-3 more reps after the 20th rep. Adjust repetition range until criteria is met but do not change the number of sets.

Health benefits:

++Strength, +++Core Stability

4. Crunch

How to:
a. Lie down on the floor facing up
b. Bend your knees so that they form a 90-degree angle
c. Lift your torso up just enough that your shoulders don't touch the floor (do not sit up completely)

Rep scheme:

***3 sets of 40 reps. each set should be difficult but you should not reach complete failure. You should be able to do 2-3 more reps after the 40th rep. Adjust repetition range until criteria is met but do not change the number of sets.

Health benefits:
+++Endurance, +++Core stability

5. Push-up plank

How to:

a. Position yourself in a push-up position
b. Lower yourself down so that you are in the first half of the push-up movement
c. Hold position

Rep scheme:

***3 sets of 60 seconds. Each set should be difficult but you should not reach complete failure. Adjust time but not number of sets if needed.

Health benefits:

+++Endurance, ++Core stability

6. Lying windmills hold

How to:
a. Lie down face-up with your arms extended and raise your legs so that they form a 90-degree angle
b. Hold the position
Rep scheme:

***3 sets of 60 seconds.

Health benefits:

+++Endurance, +++Strength

7. Spiderman plank

How to:

a. Start in a regular plank position with y our weight on the forearms and balls of your feet
b. Ensure back is straight
c. Bring right knee forward so that it touches the right elbow

d. Return to starting position
e. Repeat with left knee

Rep Scheme:

***3 sets of 10 reps. each set should be difficult but you should not reach complete failure. You should be able to do 2-3 more reps after the 10th rep. Adjust repetition range until criteria is met but do not change the number of sets.

Health benefits:

+++Strength, ++Flexibility, ++Endurance

8. Bicycle crunch

How to:

a. Lie on your back with your hands behind your head
b. Bend your legs so that they are at a 90-degree angle
c. Bring your right knee toward the left elbow and touch if possible
d. Repeat with left knee

Rep scheme:

***3 sets of 20 reps. each set should be difficult but you should not reach complete failure. You should be able to do 2-3 more reps after the 20th rep. Adjust repetition range until criteria is met but do not change the number of sets.

Health benefits:

+++Strength, +++Endurance

Delta X workout: perform exercises 1,3,5,8
Gamma workout: perform exercises 2,4,6,7

Speed/Agility Exercises

These are the exercises that you will complete on the days marked "Speed/explosiveness split" in your calendar.

1. High-intensity training(HIT) sprints

How to:

The idea is to perform 8x30 second sprints at maximum intensity with 2 minutes of rest in-between each sprint.

Health benefits:

++ Power, +++Recovery, +++Speed

2. Hill sprints (HIT)

How to:

The idea is to perform 5x 10-30 second sprints on a hill or an inclined surface with 2 minutes of rest in-between each sprint.

Health benefits:

+++Power, +++Speed

3. Hand Shuffle (core, chest, triceps)

How to:

a. Position yourself in a push-up position with hands shoulder width apart
b. Move either the right hand or left hand toward the center of the shoulder-width
c. Move the other hand toward the center. You should now be in a diamond push-up position
d. Move the first hand back to shoulder width
e. Move the second hand back to shoulder width
f. Repeat as fast as possible

Rep Scheme:

***The idea is to perform 5x 60 second sessions as fast as possible without slowing down. Exhaustion is not the goal here so if the exercise is too hard, lower sets to 30 seconds each to maintain full speed.

Health benefits:

+++Speed, ++Agility, +++Coordination

4. **Single leg hop (quads, calves)**

How to:
a. Stand shoulder width apart
b. Lift one knee up so that you are standing on one leg in a balanced position
c. Hop forward as far as you can for reps indicated below
d. Repeat with other leg

Rep Scheme:

***3x15 hops per leg. The idea is to perform the exercise as fast as possible without slowing down. Exhaustion is not the goal here so if the exercise is too hard, lower reps to maintain full speed.

Health benefits:

+++Speed, +++Agility, ++Coordination

5. Box jump (quads, glutes)

How to:
a. Stand shoulder width apart
b. Jump on the box with both feet at the same time
c. Climb back down

Rep scheme:

***3 sets of 30 box jumps. The idea is to perform the exercise as fast as possible without slowing down. Exhaustion is not the goal here so if the exercise is too hard, lower reps to maintain full speed.

Health benefits:

+++Power, +++Strength, ++Endurance

6. Clapping push-ups (chest, triceps)

How to:
a. Start in traditional push-up stance
b. Perform the push up but push off the floor as hard as possible and clap while in the air
c. Repeat

Rep scheme:

***5 sets of 5 reps. the idea is to perform the exercise as fast as possible without slowing down. Exhaustion is not the goal here so if the exercise is too hard, lower reps to maintain full speed.

Health benefits:

+++Power, +++Strength, ++Joint strength

7. Knuckle jumping push-ups (chest, triceps)

How to:
a. Start in traditional push-up stance but position the weight on your front two knuckles instead of your hand
b. Perform the push up but push off the floor as hard as possible
c. Repeat

Rep scheme:

***5 sets of 5 reps. the idea is to perform the exercise as fast as possible without slowing down. Exhaustion is not the goal here so if the exercise is too hard, lower reps to maintain full speed.

Health benefits:

+++Joint strength, +++Power

8. Later box jumps (quads, glutes)

How to:
a. Stand on the side of a box or elevated platform
b. Put the foot closest to the box on top of the box
c. Push off that foot and jump up as quickly as possible
d. Land with the right foot on the box
e. Repeat with other leg

Rep scheme:

***3 sets of 12 reps. the idea is to perform the exercise as fast as possible without slowing down. Exhaustion is not the goal here so if the exercise is too hard, lower reps to maintain full speed.

Health benefits:

+++Strength, +++Agility

Delta X workout: perform exercises 1,3,5,8
Gamma workout: perform exercises 2,4,6,7

Glossary

Active recovery: resting your muscles while staying active so that the blood flow will accelerate your recovery

Agility: the ability to be quick, accurate and effective

Coordination: the ability to employ different body parts simultaneously or perform different tasks simultaneously

Endurance: the ability to produce output over a long period of time

Failure: this is complete exhaustion, the inability to continue

Lactic threshold: this is the point at which lactate starts to accumulate in the blood which produces a burning sensation in the muscles

Power: the ability to produce the most energy in the shortest amount of time

Strength: the ability to lift higher loads for the same volume of work

CHAPTER 2: HIGH PERFORMANCE SOCCER NUTRITION

Why is nutrition important?

To maximize the effects of training sessions it's important to have a balanced diet through meals and/or juices or shakes. Improving your physical condition will require that you eat right and not fatigue sooner than expected.

What should I eat or drink before training or competing?

The ideal pre-training foods you should consume are: Lean proteins, easy to digest carbs, omega fats, vegetables and legumes, and water are and should be eaten in appropriate amounts depending on your caloric needs.

To help you prepare to compete I am including some high nutrient and high protein shakes and/or juices as well as meals to make your digestive process less of a distraction while you are performing and to have the most amount of energy before beginning.

Drinking these shakes 30-60 minutes before training will give you the best results and will keep you from feeling hungry or too full to completely relax and concentrate on the session your about to perform.

If you don't have time eat right make sure you at least drink something that will nourish your body and not just make you feel full as you need to focus on quality not quantity when it comes to what you eat and drink.

Protein

Lean proteins are very important to develop and repair muscle tissue. Lean proteins also help to normalize hormone concentrations in the body which will allow you to control your mood as well as your temper. Some of the best lean proteins you can have are:

- Turkey breast (all natural if possible).
- Lean red meat (all natural as well).
- Egg whites
- Most dairy products.
- Chicken breast (All natural).
- Quinoa
- Nuts (all varieties)

Omega fats

Omega fats are easy to obtain and very important for your body functions, especially for the brain. Omega fats are commonly found in:

- Salmon (Preferably wild, non-farmed)
- Walnuts (An easy to carry around snack)
- Flaxseeds (Blend them with any shake)
- Sardines

You will notice your brain functions improve and your brains' overall health increase. Your immune system should also get stronger which will reduce your chances of getting cancer, diabetes, and other serious health related problems.

Vegetables and Legumes

Vegetables and legumes are not given enough importance. Find a vegetable you enjoy eating and include it in your diet. It will pay off as the years go by. When you hear people talking about how important it is to have a balanced diet, they are also referring to vegetables. Some of the best vegetables and legumes to include in your daily meals are:

- Tomatoes
- Carrots
- Beets
- Kale
- Spinach
- Cabbage
- Parsley
- Broccoli
- Brussel sprouts
- Lettuce
- Radish
- Green, red, and yellow peppers
- Cucumber
- Egg plant
- Avocado

You want to make sure you get a wide variety of colors to make sure you get different vitamins and minerals.

Fruits

Fruits also contain a large amount of vitamins necessary for your body to perform to its maximum capacity. Antioxidants help your body to recover faster which is extremely important for athletes. Make sure you eat many fruits that are high on antioxidants after training or competing. Fruits provide an important source of dietary fiber which allows you to process food easier. Some of the best fruits to include in your diet are:

- Apples (green and red)
- Oranges
- Grapes (red and green)
- Bananas
- Grapefruit (A bit sour but full of antioxidants)
- Lemons and limes (In the form of juice mixed with water. I often ask for water and some slices of lemon when I go out to eat as these are wonderful antioxidants as well).
- Cherries (natural, not the sugar coated).
- Mandarins
- Watermelon
- Cantaloupe

Water

Water and hydration are very important in your body's development and can increase the amount of energy you have during the day. Drinking juices and shakes will help but are not substitutes to drinking water. The amount of water you drink will depend on the amount of cardiovascular training you do, this might be more than the usual suggested. Most people should drink at least 8 glasses of water a day but most athletes should drink 10 -14 glasses of water.

Ever since I started to carry around my gallon of water I am able to reach my "1 gallon a day" goal of water which has improved my health significantly.

Some of the benefits I have noticed and most people will notice are:

- Less or no headaches (Brain is hydrated more often)
- Improved digestion.
- Less tired during the day.
- More energy in the morning.
- Reduced amount of visible wrinkles.
- Less cramps or signs of muscle tightness. (This is a common problem for many athletes.)
- Better concentration (this will benefit you a lot when meditating).
- Decreased desire for sweets and snacks in between meals.

MUSCLE BUILDING CALENDAR

Week 1
Day 1:
Early Riser Breakfast
Snack: Blueberry Yogurt
Tuna Burger and Salad
Snack: Cherry Tomatoes with Cottage Cheese
Mexican Style Protein Bowl
Day 2:
Blueberry Lemon Pancakes
Snack: Avocado on Toast
Spicy Beefsteak Kebabs
Snack: Apple and Peanut Butter
Mediterranean Fish
Day 3:
Power Bowl
Snack: Yogurt with Tropical Fruit
Stuffed Chicken Breast with Brown Rice
Snack: Bell Pepper with Cottage Cheese
Vegan Friendly Dinner
Day 4:
Almond Milk Smoothie
Snack: Cup of Popcorn
Pancetta-wrapped Pollock with Potatoes
Snack: Yogurt with Dried Goji Berries
Garlicky Hummus
Day 5
Greek Yogurt with Flaxseeds and Apple
Snack: Rice Cake with Peanut Butter
Baked Salmon with Grilled Asparagus
Snack: Celery Sticks with Goat Cheese and Green Olives

Chicken with Avocado Salad
Day 6:
Breakfast 'Pizza'
Snack: Greek Yogurt with Strawberries
Chicken Caesar Wraps
Snack: Roasted Chickpeas
Hot Cod
Day 7:
Bell Pepper Rings with 'Frit Grits'
Snack: Nut Mix
Beef and Broccoli Noodles
Snack: Ham and Celery Sticks
Arugula Chicken Salad

Week 2
Day 1:
Whey Protein Muffins
Snack: Avocado on Toast
Shrimp and Zucchini Linguine Pasta Salad
Snack: Apple and Peanut Butter
Tofu Burger
Day 2:
Mexican Mocha Breakfast
Snack: Yogurt with Dried Goji Berries
Trout with Potato Salad
Snack: Cup of Popcorn
Chicken with Pineapple and Bell Peppers
Day 3:
Smoked Salmon and Avocado with Toast
Snack: Cherry Tomatoes with Cottage Cheese
Spiced Chicken
Snack: Blueberry Yogurt

Grilled Mushroom and Zucchini Burger
Day 4:
Fruit and Peanut Butter Smoothie
Snack: Roasted Chickpeas
Mexican Bean Chili
Snack: Greek Yogurt with Strawberries
Sweet and Sour Chicken
Day 5:
Protein-packed Scramble
Snack: Bell pepper with Cottage Cheese
Turkey Meatloaf with Whole Wheat Couscous
Snack: Yogurt with Tropical Fruit
Dijon Mustard Halibut
Day 6:
Pumpkin Pie Protein Pancakes
Snack: Ham and Celery Sticks
Mediterranean Rice
Snack: Nut Mix
Tuna Melt
Day 7:
Tuna Stuffed Bell Peppers
Snack: Celery Sticks with Goat Cheese and Green Olives
Beef Meatball Pasta with Spinach
Snack: Rice Cake with Peanut Butter
Sushi Bowl

Week 3
Day 1:
High-protein Oatmeal
Snack: Cup of Popcorn
Stuffed Eggs with Pita Bread
Snack: Apple and Peanut Butter

Tray Bake Chicken

Day 2:

Early Riser Breakfast

Snack: Avocado on Toast

Beef and Broccoli Noodles

Snack: Yogurt with Dried Goji Berries

Garlicky Hummus

Day 3:

Power Bow

Snack: Greek Yogurt with Strawberries

Chicken Caesar Wraps

Snack: Cherry Tomatoes with Goat Cheese

Mediterranean Fish

Day 4:

Blueberry Lemon Pancakes

Snack: Roasted Chickpeas

Baked Salmon with Grilled Asparagus

Snack: Blueberry Yogurt

Arugula Chicken Salad

Day 5:

Greek Yogurt with Flaxseeds and Apple

Snack: Ham and Celery Sticks

Tuna Burger and Salad

Snack: Yogurt with Tropical Fruit

Chicken with Avocado Salad

Day 6:

Bell Pepper Rings with 'Frit Grits'

Snack: Bell Peppers with Cottage Cheese

Stuffed Chicken Breast with Brown Rice

Snack: Nut Mix

Hot Cod

Day 7:

Almond Milk Smoothie
Snack: Rice Cake with Peanut Butter
Spicy Beefsteak Kebabs
Snack: Celery Sticks with Goat Cheese and Green Olives
Mexican Style Protein Bowl

Week 4
Day 1:
Breakfast 'Pizza'
Snack: Greek Yogurt with Strawberries
Pancetta-wrapped Pollock with Potatoes
Snack: Cup of Popcorn
Vegan Friendly Dinner
Day 2:
Mexican Mocha Breakfast
Snack: Cherry Tomatoes with Cottage Cheese
Mediterranean Rice
Snack: Apple and Peanut Butter
 Grilled Mushroom and Zucchini Burger
Day 3:
Fruit and Peanut Butter Smoothie
Snack: Avocado on Toast
Shrimp and Zucchini Linguine Pasta Salad
Snack: Blueberry Yogurt
Sweet and Sour Chicken
Day 4:
Pumpkin Pie Protein Pancakes
Snack: Yogurt with Dried Goji Berries
Spiced Chicken
Snack: Roasted Chickpeas
Dijon Mustard Halibut
Day 5:

Smoked Salmon and Avocado with Toast
Snack: Ham and Celery Sticks
Beef Meatball Pasta with Spinach
Snack: Nut Mix
Tofu Burger
Day 6:
High-protein Oatmeal
Snack: Bell Peppers with Cottage Cheese
Mexican Bean Chili
Snack: Yogurt with Tropical Fruit
Sushi Bowl
Day 7:
Protein-packed Scramble
Snack: Rice Cake with Peanut Butter
Trout with Potato Salad
Snack: Greek Yogurt with Strawberries
Tray Bake Chicken

2 extra days for a full month:
Day 1:
Whey Protein Muffins
Snack: Celery Sticks with Goat Cheese and Green Olives
Turkey Meatloaf with Whole Wheat Couscous
Snack: Apple and Peanut Butter
Tuna Melt
Day 2:
Tuna Stuffed Bell Peppers
Snack: Blueberry Yogurt
Stuffed Eggs with Pita Bread
Snack: Nut Mix
Chicken with Pineapple and Bell Peppers

HIGH PERFORMANCE MEAL RECIPES TO INCREASE MUSCLE

BREAKFAST
1. Early Riser Breakfast

Snap your body out of a catabolic state and into a muscle-building one with this high-protein, high-carb oven-cooked breakfast. The grapefruit and asparagus make sure you get more than half a day's worth of vitamin C.

Ingredients (1serving):
6 egg whites
½ cup cooked quinoa and brown rice mix
3 asparagus spears, sliced
½ pink grapefruit
1 small red bell pepper, sliced
1 scoop flavorless whey protein powder
1 clove garlic, crushed
olive oil spray
pepper, salt

Prep time: 10 min
Cooking time: 15-20 min

Preparation:
Heat the oven to 200C fan/ gas 6. Lightly spray a cast iron skillet with olive oil.
In a medium bowl, whisk the egg whites with a pinch of salt and pepper until frothy.
Add the cooked brown rice and quinoa to the skillet; pour in the egg whites then the asparagus pieces and the bell pepper slices.

Bake in the oven for 15-20 min or until the eggs are cooked.
Nutritional value per serving: 407kcal, 52g protein, 40g carbs (5g fiber, 8g sugar), 2g fat, 15% calcium, 12% iron, 19% magnesium, 26% vitamin A, 63% vitamin C, 48% vitamin K, 12% vitamin B1, 69% vitamin B2, 26% vitamin B9.

2. Power Bowl

A breakfast with an appropriate name, the power bowl combines high in protein egg whites with energy fueling oatmeal. The walnuts add healthy fats and the honey tops everything with a bit of sweetness.

Ingredients (1 serving):
6 egg whites
½ cup instant oatmeal, cooked
 1/8 cup walnuts
¼ cup berries
1 teaspoon raw honey
Cinnamon

Prep time: 10 min
Cooking time: 5 min

Preparation:
Whisk the egg whites until frothy then cook them in a skillet on low heat.
Combine the oatmeal and the egg whites in a bowl; add the cinnamon and raw honey and mix.
Top with berries, banana and walnuts.

Nutritional value per serving: 344kcal, 30g protein, 33g carbs (3g fiber, 23g sugar), 11g fat (2 saturated), 10% iron, 15% magnesium, 10% vitamin B1, 11% vitamin B2, 15% vitamin B5.

3. Tuna Stuffed Bell Peppers

This is a quick and nutritious recipe that provides a massive amount of B12. High in protein, tuna is an excellent breakfast option for muscle building and if you want to add some carbs to your meal, a piece of whole wheat toast is a great choice.

Ingredients (2 servings):

2 cans of tuna in water (185g), half drained

3 hard-boiled eggs

1 spring onion, finely chopped

5 small pickles, diced

Salt, pepper

4 bell peppers, halved, with the seeds cleaned

Prep time: 5 min

Cooking time: 10 min

Preparation:

Combine the tuna, eggs, spring onion, pickles and seasoning in a food processor and mix until smooth.

Fill the halves of the bell peppers with the composition and serve.

Nutritional value per serving: 480kcal, 46g protein, 16g fat (4g saturated), 8g carbs (2g fiber, 4g sugar), 28% magnesium, 94% vitamin A, 400% vitamin C, 12% vitamin E, 67% vitamin K, 18% vitamin B1, 32% vitamin B2, 90% vitamin B3, 20% vitamin B5, 56% vitamin B6, 18% vitamin B9, 284% vitamin B12.

4. Greek Yogurt with Flaxseeds and Apple

Branch out from the traditional egg white muscle-building breakfast and try some high-protein Greek Yogurt flavored with apple. Use whole flaxseeds to maximize your fiber intake and keep them in water overnight to get them soft and easily digestible.

Ingredients (1 serving):
1 cup Greek yogurt
1 apple, thinly sliced
2 tablespoons flaxseeds
¼ teaspoon cinnamon
1 teaspoon Stevia
A sprinkle of salt

Prep time: 5 min
Cooking time: 45 min

Preparation:
Preheat the oven to 190C fan/ gas 5. Place the apple slices in a non-stick pan, sprinkle them with cinnamon, Stevia and a dash of salt, cover them and bake for 45 min/ until tender. Remove them from the oven and allow them to cool for 30 min.
Place the Greek yogurt in a bowl then top with apples and flaxseeds and serve.

Nutritional value per serving: 422kcal, 22g protein, 39g carbs (7g fiber, 22 g sugar), 21g fat (8 g saturated), 14% calcium, 22% magnesium, 14% vitamin C, 24% vitamin B1, 13% vitamin B12.

5. Bell Pepper Rings with 'Fit Grits'

A tasty and special looking meal, the bell pepper rings with 'Fit Grits' fuel your muscles and give you enough energy to power through your day. Full of color and nutrients, this breakfast is high in vitamin B1.

Ingredients (1 serving):
6 egg whites
2 eggs
¼ cup brown rice farina
1 cup raw spinach
½ green bell pepper
1 cup of cherry tomatoes
Olive oil spray
Salt, pepper

Prep time: 10 min
Cooking time: 15 min

Preparation:

Whisk the egg whites with a pinch of salt and pepper until frothy. Heat some oil in a non-stick frying pan and cook the egg whites and farina. Add the spinach, mix together and cook until the spinach has wilted.

Lightly spray a skillet with olive oil and set on medium heat. Cut the bell peppers horizontally to create 2 rings, place them in the skillet and crack the eggs inside the bell peppers. Let them cook until the eggs turn white.

Place the egg-farina mixture and cooked pepper rings on a plate and serve with cherry tomatoes.

Nutritional value per serving : 495kcal, 45g protein, 45g carbs (3g fiber, 7g sugar), 11g fat (3g saturated), 9% calcium, 14% iron, 20% magnesium, 35% vitamin A, 32% vitamin C, 91% vitamin B2, 22% vitamin B5, 12% vitamin B6, 15% vitamin B12.

6. Almond Milk Smoothie

10 minutes is all you need to fix this high in vitamin D and B1 almond milk smoothie. You can fix a big batch and keep it in the freezer making this smoothie a perfect option for a quick breakfast to go.

Ingredients (2 serving):
1 cup almond milk
1 cup frozen mixed berries
1 cup spinach
1 scoop banana flavored protein powder
1 tablespoon chia seeds

Prep time: 10 min
No cooking

Preparation:
Mix all the ingredients in a blender until smooth, pour into 2 glasses and serve.

Nutritional value per serving: 295kcal, 26g protein, 32g carbs (4g fiber, 13g sugar), 9g fat, 40% calcium, 20% iron, 12% magnesium, 50% vitamin A, 40% vitamin C, 25% vitamin D, 57% vitamin E, 213% vitamin B1, 18% vitamin B9.

7. Pumpkin Pie Protein Pancakes

Forget about flour and try oat pancakes with a delicious addition of fresh pumpkin. Topple some calorie-free syrup and enjoy a high-protein breakfast that tastes as good as a cheat meal.

Ingredients (1 serving):
1/3 cup old-fashioned oats
¼ cup pumpkin
½ cup egg whites
1 scoop cinnamon protein powder
½ teaspoon cinnamon
olive oil spray

Prep time: 5 min
Cooking time: 5 min

Preparation:
Mix all the ingredients together in a bowl. Spray a medium-sized skillet with olive oil then place on medium heat.

Pour in the batter, and once you see tiny bubbles appear on the top of the pancake, flip. When each side is golden, remove the pancake and serve.

Nutritional value per serving: 335kcal, 39g protein, 37g carbs (6g fiber, 1 g sugar), 6g fat, 14% calcium, 15% iron, 26% magnesium, 60% vitamin A, 26% vitamin B1, 37% vitamin B2, 10% vitamin B5, 31% vitamin B6.

8. High-protein Oatmeal

Lasso in a hearty helping of carbs that will keep you satiated for hours, while the protein powder and almonds will deliver a protein-packed start to your day. If you prefer you oatmeal with a fruity taste, use banana flavored protein powder.

Ingredients (1 serving):
2 packets of instant oatmeal (28g packet)
¼ cup ground almonds
1 scoop of vanilla flavored whey protein powder
1 tablespoon cinnamon

Prep time: 5 min
Cooking time: 5 min

Preparation:
Pour the instant oatmeal into a bowl, mix with the protein powder and cinnamon. Add hot water and mix. Top with crushed almonds and serve.

Nutritional value per serving: 436kcal, 33g protein, 45g carbs (10g fiber, 4g sugar), 15g fat (1g saturated), 17% calcium, 19% iron, 37% magnesium, 44% vitamin E, 21% vitamin B1, 21% vitamin B2.

9. Protein-packed Scramble

Feed your muscles and push through an advanced workout with this 51g protein meal. These scrambled egg whites with vegetables and turkey sausage have the added value of being packed with carbs and overall high amounts of vitamins.

Ingredients (1 serving):
8 egg whites
2 link turkey sausages, chopped
1 large onion, diced
1 cup red bell peppers, diced
2 tomatoes, diced
2 cups raw spinach, chopped
1 teaspoon olive oil
salt and pepper

Prep time: 10 min
Cooking time: 10-15 min

Preparation:
Whisk the egg whites with a pinch of salt and pepper until frothy, then set aside.
Heat the oil in a large non-stick pan, drizzle the onions and peppers and sauté until they are tender. Season with salt and pepper. Add the turkey sausage and cook until it is golden brown then lower the heat and add the egg whites and scramble.
When the eggs are almost done, add the tomato and spinach, cook for 2 min and serve.

Nutritional value per serving: 475kcal, 51g protein, 37g carbs (10g fiber, 18g sugar), 10g fat (2g saturated), 14% calcium, 23% iron, 37% magnesium, 255% vitamin A, 516% vitamin C, 25% vitamin E, 397% vitamin K, 22% vitamin B1, 112% vitamin B2, 29% vitamin B3, 19% vitamin B5, 51% vitamin B6, 65% vitamin B9.

10. Fruit and Peanut Butter Smoothie

What better way to get your day's worth of calcium than with this strawberry flavored smoothie? High in minerals, vitamins, protein and energy fueling carbs, this smoothie is a perfect way to kick-start your day.

Ingredients (1 serving):
15 medium-sized strawberries
1 1/3 tablespoons peanut butter
85g tofu
½ cup fat free yogurt
¾ cup skim milk
1 scoop protein powder
8 ice cubes

Prep time: 5min
No cooking

Preparation:
Pour the milk into the blender then the yogurt and the rest of the ingredients. Blend until mixture is completely blended and frothy. Pour into a glass and serve.

Nutritional value per serving: 472kcal, 45g protein, 40g carbs (6g fiber, 31g sugar), 13g fat (4g saturated), 110% calcium, 35% iron, 27% magnesium, 30% vitamin A, 190% vitamin C, 11% vitamin E, 13% vitamin B1, 24% vitamin B2, 10% vitamin B5, 18% vitamin B6, 17% vitamin B9, 12% vitamin B12.

11. Whey Protein Muffins

With a healthy dose of oats and a serving of chocolate whey protein powder, these muffins are a great breakfast alternative to regular oats. Paired with a glass of milk, this meal makes sure that you get a good amount of calcium and vitamin D to go with the nice protein and carbs serving.

Ingredients (4 muffins-2 servings):
1 cup rolled oats
1 large whole egg
5 large egg whites
½ scoop chocolate whey protein powder
olive oil spray
2 cups of low fat milk, to serve

Prep time: 2 min
Cooking time: 15 min

Preparation:
Preheat the oven to 190C fan/ gas 5.
Blend all the ingredients together for 30s. Spray the muffin tin with olive oil then batter up into four muffins. Place in the oven for 15 min.

Remove from the oven, let them cool and serve with the glass of milk.

Nutritional value per serving (includes milk): 330kcal, 28g protein, 37g carbs (9g fiber, 13g sugar), 6g fat (5g saturated), 37% calcium, 22% iron, 19% magnesium, 12% vitamin A, 34% vitamin D, 44% vitamin B1, 66% vitamin B2, 25% vitamin B5, 11% vitamin B6, 24% vitamin B12.

12.Smoked Salmon and Avocado with Toast

Are you in for a tough workout and low on time? It only takes 5 min to piece together this savory breakfast. Both the salmon and avocado are high in healthy acids and this meal has enough protein and carbs to keep you motivated.

Ingredients (2 servings):
300g smoked salmon
2 medium-sized ripe avocados, stoned and peeled
Juice from ½ lemon
handful tarragon leaves, chopped
2 slices of whole wheat bread, toasted

Prep time: 5 min
No cooking time

Preparation:
Cut the avocados into chunks and toss in the lemon juice. Twist and fold the smoked salmon pieces, place them on serving plates, then scatter with the avocado and tarragon. Serve with whole wheat toast.

Nutritional value per serving: 550kcal, 34g protein, 37g carbs (12g fiber, 4g sugar), 30g fat (5g saturated), 17% iron, 24%

magnesium, 25% vitamin C, 27% vitamin E, 42% vitamin K, 16% vitamin B1, 24% vitamin B2, 55% vitamin B3, 35% vitamin B5, 40% vitamin B6, 35% vitamin B9, 81% vitamin B12.

13. Breakfast 'Pizza'

Forget about the high-calorie, non-nutritious slice of pizza and replace it with this delicious substitute. Healthy and filling, it only takes 20 min to make and it's not only high in protein, but also in minerals and vitamins.

Ingredients (1 serving):
1 small whole wheat pita
3 egg whites
1 egg
¼ cup low-fat mozzarella cheese
1 spring onion, sliced
¼ cup mushrooms, diced
¼ cup bell peppers, diced
2 slices turkey bacon, chopped
1 teaspoon olive oil
salt and pepper

Prep time: 10 min
Cooking time: 10 min

Preparation:
Whisk the eggs with a pinch of salt and pepper and add the diced vegetables.

Bend the edges of the pita bread to create a bowl. Brush both sides with the olive oil and place the pita bread on the grill, dome side down. Cook until golden then flip it on the other side. Pour the egg mix into the pita and cook until the eggs are nearly done, add the turkey bacon, spring onion and cheese. Cook until the cheese had melted and serve.

Nutritional value per serving: 350kcal, 33g protein, 12g carbs (3g fiber, 4g sugar), 15g fat (6 saturated), 32% calcium, 19% iron, 15% magnesium, 36% vitamin A, 88% vitamin C, 72% vitamin K, 21% vitamin B1, 71% vitamin B2, 22% vitamin B3, 14% vitamin B5, 21% vitamin B6, 25% vitamin B9, 29% vitamin B12.

14. Mexican Mocha Breakfast

Top your favorite cup of oats with a healthy serving of almond milk and enjoy a quickly-made high-fiber breakfast. The cayenne pepper is perfect for adding a little oomph to your oatmeal.

Ingredients (1 serving):
½ cup rolled oats
1 scoop chocolate protein powder
½ tablespoon cinnamon
½ teaspoon cayenne pepper
1 cup unsweetened almond milk
1 tablespoon unsweetened cocoa powder

Prep time: 5 min
Cooking time: 3 min

Preparation:
Mix all the ingredients in a microwave-safe bowl. Heat in the microwave for 2 ½ -3 min then serve.

Nutritional value per serving: 304kcal, 27g protein, 38g carbs (8g fiber, 3g sugar), 7g fat, 32% calcium, 15% iron, 25% magnesium, 10% vitamin A, 25% vitamin D, 51% vitamin E, 12% vitamin B1.

15.Blueberry Lemon Pancakes

A warm, filling breakfast, this blueberry pancake enriched by the lemony flavor is a simple and tasty way of getting that high-powered meal that you need to start your day. Spread a tablespoon of Greek yogurt on top of your pancake if you like.

Ingredients (1 serving):
1/3 cup oat bran
5 egg whites
½ cup blueberries
1 scoop flavorless whey protein powder
½ teaspoon baking soda
1 teaspoon grated lemon peel
1 tablespoon lemon drink mix
olive oil spray

Prep time: 5 min
Cooking time: 5 min

Preparation:
Combine all the ingredients in a large bowl, mix and whisk until smooth.
Cook the batch in a sprayed skilled on medium-high temperature until bubbles form on the surface. Flip over and cook until each side is dark golden brown. Remove the pancake and serve.

Nutritional value per serving: 340kcal, 47g protein, 37g carbs (6g fiber, 14g sugar), 5g fat, 10% iron, 25% magnesium, 12% vitamin C, 19% vitamin K, 26% vitamin B1, 58% vitamin B2.

LUNCH

16. Mediterranean Rice

Turn the tired can of tuna into a delicious dish that is a perfect starter for an afternoon of exercise. The high amount of carbs will fuel a thorough workout and the protein will make sure that your muscles recuperate from the effort.

Ingredients (1 serving):
1 can of tuna in oil, drained
100g brown rice
¼ avocado, chopped
¼ red onion, sliced
juice from ½ lemon
salt and pepper

Prep time: 5 min
Cooking time: 20 min

Preparation:
Boil the brown rice for approximately 20 min then place in a bowl with the onion, tuna and avocado. Add the lemon juice and mix all the ingredients. Season with salt and pepper to taste and serve.

Nutritional value per serving: 590kcal, 32g protein, 80g carbs (7g fiber, 1g sugar), 14g fat (5g saturated), 22% iron, 52% magnesium, 101% vitamin D, 18% vitamin E, 107% vitamin K,

32% vitamin B1, 134% vitamin B3, 26% vitamin B5, 39% vitamin B6, 15% vitamin B9, 63% vitamin B12.

17.Spiced Chicken

Chicken is perfect for a high protein muscle building meal. High in nutrients across the board, this simple, tasty meal can be paired with a serving of your choice of carbs.

Ingredients (2 servings):
3 boneless chicken breasts cut in half
175g low-fat yogurt
5cm piece cucumber, finely chopped
2 tablespoons Thai red curry paste
2 tablespoons cilantro, chopped
2 cups raw spinach, to serve.

Prep time: 5 min
Cooking time: 35-40 min

Preparation:
Preheat the oven to 190C fan/ gas 5. Put the chicken in a dish in one layer. Blend a third of the yogurt, the curry paste and two thirds of the cilantro, add salt and pour over the chicken, making sure the meat is evenly coated. Leave for 30 min (or in the fridge overnight).
Lift the chicken onto a rack in a roasting tin for 35-40 min, until golden.
Heat water in a pan and wilt the spinach.

Mix the rest of the yogurt and cilantro, add the cucumber and stir. Pour the mix over the chicken and serve with the cooked spinach.

Nutritional value per serving: 275kcal, 43g protein, 8g carbs (1g fiber, 8g sugar), 3g fat (1g saturated), 20% calcium, 15% iron, 25% magnesium, 56% vitamin A, 18% vitamin C, 181% vitamin K, 16% vitamin B1, 26% vitamin B2, 133% vitamin B3, 25% vitamin B5, 67% vitamin B6, 19% vitamin B9, 22% vitamin B12.

18.Stuffed Eggs with Pita Bread

Get your fill of omega-3 fatty acids with this rich salmon dish. High in vitamins and minerals, this filling meal is a great way of boosting yourself with energy and powering through your day.

Ingredients (2 servings):
1 canned salmon in water (450g)
2 eggs
1 large spring onions, finely chopped
2 large leafs of lettuce
10 cherry tomatoes
1 tablespoon Greek yogurt
a large whole wheat pita bread, cut in half
sea salt and pepper

Prep time: 10 min
Cooking time: 10 min

Preparation:
Boil the eggs, peel them and slice them in half then remove the yolks and place them in a bowl.

Add the canned salmon, 1 tablespoon of yogurt, the spring onion and the seasonings to the bowl. Mix all the ingredients together and stuff the egg whites. Serve with pita bread stuffed with lettuce and tomatoes.

Nutritional value per serving: 455kcal, 45g protein, 24g carbs (3g fiber, 2g sugar), 36g fat (10g saturated), 59% calcium, 22% iron, 21% magnesium, 30% vitamin A, 24% vitamin C, 43% vitamin K, 11% vitamin B1, 36% vitamin B2, 60% vitamin B3, 20% vitamin B5, 41% vitamin B6, 20% vitamin B9, 20% vitamin B12.

19. Chicken Caesar Wraps

These chicken wraps make a great portable meal that will make sure that you keep your protein levels high throughout the day. Throw in some baby spinach and make a more green friendly meal.

Ingredients (1 serving):
85g chicken breast, baked
2 whole wheat tortillas
1 cup lettuce
50g non-fat yogurt
1 teaspoon anchovy paste
1 teaspoon dry mustard powder
1 clove garlic, cooked
½ medium cucumber, chopped

Prep time: 5 min
No cooking

Preparation:

Combine the anchovy paste, garlic and yogurt then toss and coat the lettuce and cucumbers. Split the mix in 2, add to the tortillas and then place half the chicken in each tortilla. Wrap up and serve.

Nutritional value per serving (2 tortillas): 460kcal, 41g protein, 57g carbs (7g fiber, 9g sugar), 10g fat (2g saturated), 11% calcium, 22% vitamin K, 13% vitamin B2, 59% vitamin B3, 12% vitamin B5, 29% vitamin B6, 10% vitamin B12.

20.Baked Salmon with Grilled Asparagus

A classic dish, made more interesting by a marinade of lemon juice and mustard, this grilled salmon goes well with the garlicky asparagus spears. Treat yourself to a great combination of protein and vitamins.

Ingredients (1 serving):
140g wild salmon
1 ½ cup asparagus
Marinade:
1 tablespoon garlic, minced
1 tablespoon Dijon mustard
lemon juice from ½ lemon
1 teaspoon olive oil

Prep time: 5 min
Cooking time: 15 min

Preparation:
Preheat oven to 200C fan/ gas 6.

In a bowl, mix the lemon juice, half the garlic, olive oil and mustard, pour the marinade over the salmon and make sure it is completely covered. Place the marinating salmon in the fridge for at least one hour.

Cut the bottom stems off the asparagus spears. Set a nonstick skillet on medium/high heat, toss the asparagus with the remaining garlic and sear for about 5 min, rolling the asparagus on all sides.

Place the salmon on a baking sheet and bake for 10 min then serve with the grilled asparagus.

Nutritional value: 350kcal, 43g protein, 7g carbs (5g fiber, 1 g sugar), 16g fat (1 saturated), 17% iron, 20% magnesium, 48% vitamin A, 119% vitamin C, 17% vitamin E, 288% vitamin K, 39% vitamin B1, 60% vitamin B2, 90% vitamin B3, 33% vitamin B5, 74% vitamin B6, 109% vitamin B9, 75% vitamin B12.

21. Beef Meatball Pasta with Spinach

A high-protein pasta meal that makes the most of the beef and spinach pairing. Not only is it all-round vitamin packed, but it also contains a hearty amount of magnesium which helps regulate muscle contraction.

Ingredients (2 servings):
For meatballs:
170g lean ground beef
½ cup raw spinach, shredded
1 tablespoon minced garlic
¼ cup red onion, diced
1 teaspoon cumin
sea salt and pepper
For Pasta:

100g wheat spinach pasta
10 cherry tomatoes
2 cups raw spinach
¼ cup marinara
2 tablespoons low-fat parmesan cheese

Prep time: 15 min
Cooking time: 30 min

Preparation:
Preheat oven to 200C/ gas 6.
Mix together the ground beef, raw spinach, garlic, red onion and salt and pepper to taste. Mix thoroughly with your hands until the spinach is completely mixed into the meat.
Form two or three meatballs, roughly the same size then place them on a baking sheet in the oven for 10-12 minutes.
Cook the pasta according to the instructions on the pack. Drain the pasta and stir in the tomatoes, spinach and cheese. Add the meatballs and serve.
Nutritional value per serving: 470kcal, 33g protein, 50g carbs (6g fiber, 5g sugar), 12g fat (5g saturated), 17% calcium, 28% iron, 74% magnesium, 104% vitamin A, 38% vitamin C, 11% vitamin E, 361% vitamin K, 16% vitamin B1, 20% vitamin B2, 45% vitamin B3, 11% vitamin B5, 45% vitamin B6, 35% vitamin B9, 37% vitamin B12.

22. Stuffed Chicken Breast with Brown Rice

Brown rice is an excellent way of introducing quality carbs to your diet. Couple it with high-protein chicken breast and some vegetables and you have a delicious power lunch.

Ingredients (1 serving):
170g chicken breast
½ cup raw spinach
50g brown rice
1 spring onion, diced
1 tomato, sliced
1 tablespoon feta cheese

Prep time: 10 min
Cooking time: 30 min

Preparation:
Preheat the oven to 190C fan/ gas 5.
Slice the chicken breast down the middle to make it look like a butterfly. Season the chicken with salt and pepper, then open it and layer spinach, feta cheese and tomato slices on one side. Fold the chicken breast and use a toothpick to hold it closed then bake for 20 min.
Boil the brown rice then add the garlic and chopped onion. Fill a plate with brown rice, place the chicken on top and serve.
Nutritional value per serving: 469kcal, 48g protein, 46g carbs (5g fiber, 6g sugar), 8g fat (5g saturated), 22% calcium, 18% iron, 38% magnesium, 55% vitamin A, 43% vitamin C, 169% vitamin K, 28% vitamin B1, 28% vitamin B2, 103% vitamin B3, 28% vitamin B5, 70% vitamin B6, 23% vitamin B9, 17% vitamin B12.

23. Shrimp and Zucchini Linguine Pasta Salad

A cheat pasta meal with a serving of shredded zucchini and steamed shrimp flavored with all manners of sesame. This combination of ingredients makes for a light lunch with a high-protein content.

Ingredients (1 serving):
170g steamed shrimp
1 large zucchini, chopped
¼ cup red onion, sliced
1 cup bell peppers, sliced
1 tablespoon roasted Tahini butter
1 teaspoon sesame oil
1 teaspoon sesame seeds

Prep time: 10 min
No cooking

Preparation:
Cut the zucchini using a shredder in order to make raw linguine.
In a bowl, mix tahini and sesame oil.
Place all the ingredients in a large bowl, pour the Tahini sauce and toss it to make sure all sides are covered in sauce. Sprinkle some sesame seeds and serve.
Nutritional value per serving: 420kcal, 45g protein, 26g carbs (10g fiber, 12g sugar), 18g fat (2g saturated), 19% calcium, 47% iron, 48% magnesium, 33% vitamin A, 303% vitamin C, 17% vitamin E, 31% vitamin K, 38% vitamin B1, 36% vitamin B2, 38% vitamin B3, 13% vitamin B5, 66% vitamin B6, 35% vitamin B9, 42% vitamin B12.

24. Turkey Meatloaf with Whole Wheat Couscous

Cooked in a muffin pan, this turkey meatloaf makes sure that you minimize you saturated fats intake. Mix it up a little by adding bell pepper or mushrooms instead of onion into the meatballs and by seasoning with a pinch of ground garlic.

Ingredients (1 serving):
140g lean ground turkey
¾ cup red onions, diced
1 cup raw spinach
1/3 cup low sodium marinara sauce
½ cup whole wheat couscous, boiled
choice of seasoning: Parsley, Basil, Coriander
pepper, salt
olive oil spray

Prep time: 5 min
Cooking time: 20 min

Preparation:
Preheat oven to 200C fan/ gas 6.
Season turkey with your choice of seasoning and add the diced onions.
Light spray your muffin pan with olive oil, place the ground turkey inside the muffin holders. Top each turkey meatball with 1 tablespoon marinara sauce, then place in the oven and bake for 8-10 min.
Serve with couscous.
Nutritional value per serving: 460kcal, 34g protein, 53g carbs (4g fiber, 7g sugar), 12g fat (4g saturated), 12% calcium, 15% iron, 10% magnesium, 16% vitamin A, 15% vitamin C, 11% vitamin E, 16% vitamin K, 11% vitamin B1, 25% vitamin B3, 16% vitamin B6, 11% vitamin B9.

25. Tuna Burger and Salad

The tuna burger is high in protein and carbs, making it an excellent choice for a workout day meal. Fix it differently every time and keep it interesting by switching between vegetables and seasoning your salad dressing.

Ingredients (1 serving):
1 canned chunk tuna (165g)
1 egg white
½ cup chopped mushrooms
2 cups lettuce, shredded
¼ cup dried oats
1 teaspoon olive oil
1 tablespoons low-fat salad dressing (of preference)
small bunch of oregano, chopped
1 whole wheat medium roll cut in half

Prep time: 10 min
Cooking time: 10 min

Preparation:
Mix together the egg white, tuna, dry oats, oregano and form a patty.
Heat the oil in a non-stick pan on medium heat, place the patty on and flip it to make sure it cooks on both sides.
Cut the whole wheat roll in half, horizontally, place the patty between the 2 pieces.
Mix the vegetables in a bowl, add the salad dressing and serve next to the tuna burger.
Nutritional value per serving: 560kcal, 52g protein, 76g carbs (13g fiber, 7g sugar), 10g fat (1g saturated), 11% calcium, 35%

iron, 38% magnesium, 16% vitamin A, 16% vitamin K, 35% vitamin B1, 33% vitamin B2, 24% vitamin B3, 28% vitamin B5, 41% vitamin B6, 21% vitamin B9, 82% vitamin B12.

26.Spicy Beefsteak Kebabs

This spicy kebab is served with a side of baked potato, making it not only a muscle building meal but also a great way of introducing eyesight protecting vitamin A to your diet. Add a tablespoon of low-fat yogurt to your potato to make it more refreshing.

Ingredients (1 serving):
140g lean beef flank steak
200g sweet potato
1 bell pepper, chopped
½ medium zucchini, chopped
minced garlic
pepper, salt

Prep time: 15 min
Cooking time: 55 min

Preparation:
Preheat oven to 200C fan/ gas 6. Wrap the sweet potato in a foil, place in the oven and bake for 45 min.
Cut the flank steak into small pieces, season with salt, pepper and garlic. Assemble the kebab, alternating between beef, zucchini and bell pepper.
Place the kebab on a baking sheet and bake for 10 min. Serve with the sweet potato.

Nutritional value per serving: 375kcal, 38g protein, 49g carbs (9g fiber, 12g sugar), 4g fat (1g saturated), 24% iron, 27% magnesium, 581% vitamin A, 195% vitamin C, 21% vitamin K, 22% vitamin B1, 28% vitamin B2, 61% vitamin B3, 28% vitamin B5, 92% vitamin B6, 20% vitamin B9, 30% vitamin B12.

27.Trout with Potatoes Salad

Want to make sure that you are not lacking in vitamin B12? Try this hearty portion of trout, paired with a nutrient and vitamin packed fresh-tasting potato salad.

Ingredients (2 servings):
2*140g trout fillets
250g waxy potatoes, halved
4 teaspoons yogurt
4 teaspoons reduced-fat mayonnaise
1 tablespoon capers, rinsed
4 small cornichons, sliced
2 spring onions, finely sliced
¼ cucumber, diced
1 lemon, zest from ½

Prep time: 10 min
Cooking time: 20 min

Preparation:
Boil the potatoes in salted water for 15 min until they are just tender. Drain and rinse under cold water, then drain again.
Heat the grill.

Mix the mayonnaise and yogurt and season with some lemon juice. Stir the mix into the potatoes with the capers, most of the spring onion, cucumber and cornichons. Scatter the salad with the rest of the onions.

Season the trout, grill on a baking sheet, skin-side down, until just cooked. Scatter with the lemon zest and serve with the potato salad.

Nutritional value per serving: 420kcal, 38g protein, 28g carbs (3g fiber, 6g sugar), 13g fat (3g saturated), 12% calcium, 11% iron, 22% magnesium, 29% vitamin C, 59% vitamin K, 21% vitamin B1, 18% vitamin B2, 12% vitamin B3, 22% vitamin B5, 43% vitamin B6, 18% vitamin B9, 153% vitamin B12.

28.Mexican Bean Chili

A high in protein midday meal, this dish is a great way of getting 1/3 of your daily required amount of fiber. Though it has enough nutrients to be a stand-alone meal, it can also be served on top of a bed of brown rice.

Ingredients (2 servings):
250g minced beef
200g caned baked beans
75ml beef stock
½ onion, diced
½ red pepper, diced
1 teaspoon chipotle paste
1 teaspoon olive oil
½ teaspoon chili powder
1 cup brown rice, boiled (optional)
coriander leaves, to serve

Prep time: 5 min

Cooking time: 45 min

Preparation:
Heat the oil in a non-stick pan over medium heat then fry the onion and red pepper until softened. Increase the heat, add the chili powder and cook for 2 min before adding the minced beef. Cook until browned and all the liquid has evaporated.

Tip in the beef stock, baked beans and chipotle paste. Simmer over a low heat for 20 min, then season and scatter with coriander leaves and serve with the boiled rice.

Nutritional value per serving (without rice): 402kcal, 34g protein, 19g carbs (5g fiber, 10g sugar), 14g fat (5g saturated), 29% iron, 15% magnesium, 42% vitamin C, 11% vitamin B1, 16% vitamin B2, 34% vitamin B3, 40% vitamin B6, 18% vitamin B9, 52% vitamin B12.

½ cup of rice: 108kcal

29. Beef and Broccoli Noodles

A convenient, tasty dish, the beef and broccoli noodles take only 20 min to prepare, making it a great choice for a busy day. You can serve with a few slices of red chili for some extra spice.

Ingredients (2 servings):
2 cups egg noodles
200g beef stir-fry strips
1 spring onion, sliced
½ head broccoli, small florets
1 teaspoon sesame oil
For the sauce:
1 ½ tablespoons low-salt soy sauce
1 teaspoon tomato ketchup
1 garlic clove, crushed

1 tablespoon oyster sauce
¼ knob ginger, finely grated
1 teaspoon white wine vinegar

Prep time: 10 min
Cooking time: 10 min

Preparation:
Mix the ingredients for the sauce. Boil the noodles according to the pack instructions. Tip in the broccoli when they are almost ready. Leave for a few minutes then drain the noodles and broccoli.

Heat the oil in a wok until very hot then stir-fry the beef for 2-3 minutes until browned. Tip the sauce, stir, and let it simmer for a few moments then turn off the heat.

Stir the beef into the noodles, scatter with the spring onion and serve immediately.

Nutritional value per serving: 352kcal, 33g protein, 39g carbs (5g fiber, 5g sugar), 9g fat (2g saturated), 20% iron, 20% magnesium, 20% vitamin A, 224% vitamin C, 214% vitamin K, 14% vitamin B1, 19% vitamin B2, 43% vitamin B3, 18% vitamin B5, 50% vitamin B6, 31% vitamin B9, 23% vitamin B12.

30.Pancetta-wrapped Pollock with Potatoes

This light and fresh-tasting dish provides a lot of energy and is high in protein, making it an ideal option for a midday meal. The pollock can be substituted for another sustainable white fish, while the olives can be replaced by sundried tomatoes.

Ingredients (2 servings):
2* 140g pollock fillets

4 slices pancetta
300g new potatoes
100g green beans
30g kalamata olives
juice and zest from 1 lemon
2 tablespoons olive oil
a few tarragon sprigs, leaves picked

Prep time: 10 min
Cooking time 15 min

Preparation:
Heat oven to 200C fan/ gas 6. Boil the potatoes for 10-12 min until tender, add the beans for the final 2-3 min. Drain well, slice the potatoes in half and tip into a baking dish. Toss with the olives, lemon zest and oil and season well.
Season the fish and wrap with the pancetta then place it on top of the potatoes. Bake for 10-12 min until cooked through, then add the lemon juice, scatter with tarragon and serve.
Nutritional value per serving: 525kcal, 46g protein, 36g carbs (5g fiber, 3g sugar), 31g fat (8g saturated), 10% iron, 31% magnesium, 63% vitamin C, 18% vitamin K, 15% vitamin B1, 13% vitamin B2, 14% vitamin B3, 25% vitamin B6, 73% vitamin B12.

DINNER
31.Sushi Bowl

A low-calorie sushi bowl that substitutes rice for cauliflower flavored with garlic, soy sauce and lime juice for extra taste. Use the seaweed sheets to wrap the veggies and salmon and make a mini roll.

Ingredients (2 servings):
170g smoked salmon
1 medium-sized avocado
½ head cauliflower, steamed and chopped
1/3 cup carrot, shredded
½ teaspoon cayenne
1.2 teaspoon garlic powder
1 tablespoon low-sodium soy sauce
2 seaweed sheets
Juice from ½ lime

Prep time: 10 min
No cooking

Preparation:
Place the cauliflower, carrots, soy sauce, garlic, lime juice and cayenne in a food processor. Stop blending before the mix turns into a paste. Serve next to the salmon and seaweed sheets.
Nutritional value per serving: 272kcal, 20g protein, 13g carbs (7g fiber, 4g sugar), 16g fat (1g saturated), 10% iron, 14% magnesium, 73% vitamin A, 88% vitamin C, 13% vitamin E, 40% vitamin K, 18% vitamin B1, 15% vitamin B2, 31% vitamin B3, 21% vitamin B5, 31% vitamin B6, 26% vitamin B9, 45% vitamin B12.

32. Sweet and Sour Chicken

The sweet and sour chicken is a simple, delicious recipe that has a place in every fit kitchen. It is high in protein and vitamins and goes well with steamed broccoli florets.

Ingredients (2 servings):
300g chicken breasts cut into bite-sized pieces

1 teaspoon garlic salt
¼ cup low sodium chicken broth
¼ cup white vinegar
¼ no-calorie sweetener
¼ teaspoon black pepper
1 teaspoon low-sodium soy sauce
3 teaspoons low-sugar ketchup
arrowroot
400g broccoli florets, steamed

Prep time: 10 min
Cooking time 15 min

Preparation:
Place the chicken in a large bowl and season with the garlic, pepper and salt, turning to coat. Cook the chicken over medium/high heat until done.
In the meantime, whisk together the chicken broth, sweetener, vinegar, ketchup and soy sauce in a sauce pan, bring the mix to a boil and turn to low heat. Add the arrowroot a little at a time and whisk briskly. Keep stirring for a few minutes.
Pour sauce over the cooked chicken and serve with a side of steamed broccoli.
Nutritional value per serving: 250kcal, 40g protein, 14g carbs (6g fiber, 4g sugar), 2g fat, 11% calcium, 14% iron, 20% magnesium, 24% vitamin A, 303% vitamin C, 254% vitamin K, 17% vitamin B1, 21% vitamin B2, 90% vitamin B3, 24% vitamin B5, 58% vitamin B6, 33% vitamin B9.

33.Garlicky Hummus

You only need 5 min to make this healthy, delicious meal. It is chock-full with magnesium and has a decent amount of protein considering the recipe is meatless. Grab a whole wheat tortilla and make this meal to go.

Ingredients (3 servings):
1*400g canned chickpeas (save1/4 of the liquid)
¼ cup tahini
¼ cup lemon juice
1 clove garlic
1 tablespoon olive oil
¼ teaspoon ground ginger
¼ teaspoon ground cumin
2 spring onions, finely chopped
1 tomato, chopped

Prep time: 5 min
No cooking

Preparation:
Place the chickpeas, liquid, tahini, lemon juice, olive oil, garlic, cumin and ginger in a food processor and blend until smooth.
Stir in the tomato and scallions and season with salt and pepper.
Serve next to slices of bell pepper.
Nutritional value per serving: 324kcal, 11g protein, 21g carbs (7g fiber, 1g sugar), 17g fat (2g saturated), 22% calcium, 54% iron, 135% magnesium, 10% vitamin A, 12% vitamin C, 33% vitamin K, 122% vitamin B1, 12% vitamin B2, 44% vitamin B3, 11% vitamin B5, 12% vitamin B6, 40% vitamin B9.

34.Chicken with Pineapple and Bell Peppers

Take a break from the usual chicken recipes and try this version with sweet, fresh pineapple. High in vitamin B3 and protein, this meal is also an important source of carbs. In tone with the change of pace, you can substitute the rice for quinoa.

Ingredients (1 serving):
140g boneless chicken breast,
1 tablespoon mustard
½ cup fresh pineapple, diced
½ cup bell peppers, diced
50g brown rice
Coconut oil spray
1 teaspoon cumin
salt and pepper

Prep time: 5 min
Cooking time: 15 min

Preparation:
Cut the chicken into small pieces then rub the mustard on the pieces and season with salt, pepper and cumin.
Set a skillet on medium heat and lightly spray with coconut oil, add the chicken and cook on all sides. When the chicken is almost finished, increase the heat and toss in the pineapple pieces and bell peppers, cook and make sure that all sides are brown. This should take 3-5 min.
Boil the brown rice and serve next to the chicken.
Nutritional value per serving: 377kcal, 37g protein, 50g carbs (6g fiber, 10g sugar), 1g fat, 12% iron, 33% magnesium, 168% vitamin C, 26% vitamin B1, 13% vitamin B2, 96% vitamin B3, 22% vitamin B5, 65% vitamin B6, 10% vitamin B9.

35. Mexican Style Protein Bowl

Give yourself a break from meat and throw these ingredients together for a tasty alternative to the usual. You can skip the fried fat and unhealthy calories and still get the flavor of a Mexican meal.

Ingredients:
1/3 cup cooked black beans
½ cup cooked brown rice
2 tablespoons salsa
¼ avocado, sliced

Prep time: 5 min
No cooking

Preparation:
Combine all the ingredients in a bowl and serve.
Nutritional value per serving: 307kcal, 11g protein, 48g carbs (11g fiber, 1g sugar), 7g fat (1g sugar), 26% magnesium, 13% vitamin K, 16% vitamin B1, 11% vitamin B3, 17% vitamin B6, 30% vitamin B9.

36. Arugula Chicken Salad

The arugula leaves add satisfaction to this sweet and super healthy salad. Bountiful in vegetables and quality protein source, this meal can be enriched with a simple dressing of low-fat yogurt and garlic.

Ingredients (1 serving):
120g chicken breast
5 baby carrots, chopped

¼ red cabbage, chopped
½ cup arugula
1 tablespoon sunflower seeds
1 teaspoon olive oil

Prep time: 10 min
Cooking time: 10 min

Preparation:
Cut the chicken into bite-sized cubes. Heat the olive oil in a non-stick pan and fry the chicken until it is cooked. Set aside and allow cooling.
Place the carrots, arugula and cabbage in a large bowl. Top the salad with the cooled chicken and sunflower seeds and serve.
Nutritional value per serving: 311kcal, 30g protein, 9g carbs (1g fiber), 13g fat (1g saturated), 11% iron, 22% magnesium, 150% vitamin A, 25% vitamin C, 29% vitamin E, 32% vitamin K, 23% vitamin B1, 10% vitamin B2, 72% vitamin B3, 11% vitamin B5, 49% vitamin B6, 17% vitamin B9.

37. Dijon Mustard Halibut

This tangy halibut meal is a fast-and-easy way to get a hearty dose of protein. It's low in carbs and high in vitamins, making it a perfect choice for supper. The low calorie count allows you to double the sauce if you are feeling indulgent.

Ingredients (2 servings):
220g halibut
¼ onion, diced
1 red pepper, diced
1 clove garlic

1 tablespoon Dijon mustard
1 teaspoon Worcestershire sauce
1 teaspoon olive oil
juice from 1 lemon
a bunch of parsley
2 large carrots cut into sticks
1 cup broccoli florets
1 cup mushrooms, sliced

Prep time: 10 min
Cooking time: 20 min

Preparation:
Place the red pepper, garlic, parsley, mustard, onion Worcestershire sauce, lemon juice and olive oil in a food processor.
Place the fish, sauce and the rest of the vegetables in a large parchment baking bag. Bake at 190C fan/ gas 5 for 20 min then serve.
Nutritional value per serving: 225kcal, 33g protein, 12g carbs (3g fiber, 5g sugar), 5g fat (1g saturated), 11% calcium, 10% iron, 35% magnesium, 180% vitamin A, 77% vitamin C, 71% vitamin K, 13% vitamin B1, 19% vitamin B2, 51% vitamin B3, 14% vitamin B5, 34% vitamin B6, 15% vitamin B9, 25% vitamin B12.

38.Tray Bake Chicken

Quick, easy and tasty, this dish should be a summer staple in your kitchen since there is no shortage of fresh cherry tomatoes. The pesto adds a refreshing flavor to a simply seasoned chicken breast.

Ingredients (2 servings):
300g chicken breast
300g cherry tomatoes
2 tablespoons pesto
1 tablespoon olive oil
salt, pepper

Prep time: 5 min
Cooking time: 15 min

Preparation:
Place the chicken breast in a roasting tray, season, drizzle with the olive oil then grill for 10 min. Add the cherry tomatoes and grill for another 5 min until the chicken is cooked. Spread pesto over the top and serve next to the cherry tomatoes.
Nutritional value per serving: 312kcal, 36g protein, 7g carbs (2g fiber, 5g sugar), 19g fat (4g saturated), 15% magnesium, 25% vitamin A, 34% vitamin C, 11% vitamin E, 20% vitamin K, 10% vitamin B1, 88% vitamin B3, 13% vitamin B5, 33% vitamin B6.

39. Tofu burger

Tofu has all of the essential amino acids, and that makes it a perfect substitute for meat. The caramelized onions with chili flakes and Sriracha, paired with the teriyaki infused tofu will delight your taste buds.

Ingredients (1 serving):
85g tofu (extra firm)
1 tablespoon teriyaki marinade
1 tablespoon Sriracha
1 lettuce leaf

30g carrot, shredded
¼ red onion, sliced
½ teaspoon red chili flakes
1 medium-sized whole wheat roll

Prep time: 5 min
Cooking time: 10 min

Preparation:
Heat the grill.
Marinate the tofu in teriyaki marinade, red chili flakes and Sriracha then grill it for 3-5 min on each side.
Fry the red onion in a non-stick pan until caramelized.
Cut the roll in half until you can open it like a book. Stuff the roll with the grilled tofu, caramelized onion, carrots and lettuce and serve.
Nutritional value per serving: 194kcal, 11g protein, 28g carbs (5g fiber, 8g sugar), 5g fat (1g saturated), 21% calcium, 14% iron, 19% magnesium, 95% vitamin A, 10% vitamin B1, 14% vitamin B6.

40. Hot Cod

High in protein and healthy fats and low in carbs, this super spicy cod will give a jolt for the rest of your day. Serve it with a bit of brown rice if you need a carb boost for an evening workout and add 2 more peppers if you feel you can handle more spice.

Ingredients (2 servings):
340g white cod
10 cherry tomatoes, halved
2 jalapeno peppers, sliced

2 tablespoons olive oil
sea salt
chili powder

Prep time: 5 min
Cooking time: 10 min

Preparation:
Heat the oil in a non-stick pan. Coat the cod in salt and chili powder, add to the pan and cook for 10 min on medium heat. Toss in the peppers 1-2 min before the fish is cooked through. Serve with cherry tomatoes.
Nutritional value per serving: 279kcal, 30g protein, 6g carbs (1g fiber, 1 g sugar), 16g fat (2g saturated), 11% magnesium, 17% vitamin A, 38% vitamin C, 26% vitamin E, 33% vitamin K, 24% vitamin B3, 43% vitamin B6, 26% vitamin B12.

41.Grilled Mushroom and Zucchini Burger

The Portobello mushrooms have a thick, meaty texture that makes them a favorite among vegetarians and meat lovers alike. Indulge in nature's burger and get a load of minerals and vitamins at a minimal calorie cost.

Ingredients (1 serving):
1 large portabella mushroom cap
¼ small zucchini, sliced
1 teaspoon roasted bell peppers
1 slice of low fat cheese
4 spinach leaves
olive oil spray
1 medium-sized whole wheat roll

Prep time: 5 min
Cooking time: 5 min

Preparation:
Heat the grill. Spray the mushroom cap with olive oil then grill both mushroom and zucchini slices.
Cut the roll in half, horizontally, then place the ingredients in layers on one half and cover with the other. Serve immediately.
Nutritional value per serving: 185kcal, 12g protein, 24g carbs (4g fiber, 5g sugar), 4g fat (1g saturated), 21% calcium, 17% iron, 20% magnesium, 78% vitamin A, 28% vitamin C, 242% vitamin K, 15% vitamin B1, 37% vitamin B2, 26% vitamin B3, 16% vitamin B5, 16% vitamin B6, 31% vitamin B9.

42.Mediterranean Fish

What better way to reach your daily B12 requirement than with a dish bursting of Mediterranean flavors? The rest of the vitamins and minerals are also well represented and the protein count is at a good amount for a light supper.

Ingredients (2 servings):
200g fresh trout
2 medium-sized tomatoes
3 teaspoons capers
½ red bell pepper, chopped
1 garlic clove, chopped
10 green olives, sliced
¼ onion, chopped
½ cup spinach
1 tablespoon olive oil

salt and pepper

Prep time: 10 min
Cooking time: 15 min

Preparation:
Heat a large pan over medium heat; add whole tomatoes, garlic and olive oil. Cover and let it simmer for a few minutes until the tomatoes begin to soften.
Add the onion, bell pepper, olives, capers, salt and pepper (and a little water if necessary). Cover and let it simmer until the tomatoes have broken down and the bell pepper and onion have softened.
Add the trout, cover and poach for 5-7 min.
Add the spinach at the last minute then serve.
Nutritional value per serving: 305kcal, 24g protein, 7g carbs (1g fiber, 4g sugar), 11g fat (3g saturated), 10% calcium, 12% magnesium, 36% vitamin A, 56% vitamin C, 62% vitamin K, 13% vitamin B1, 33% vitamin B3, 12% vitamin B5, 25% vitamin B6, 15% vitamin B9, 105% vitamin B12.

43.Vegan friendly dinner

A vegan friendly meal with a good amount of protein and vitamins. Give your palate the taste it deserves with this sweet and spicy sauce that flavors a filling amount of tofu and is easy to make.

Ingredients (2 servings):
340g tofu
¼ cup soy sauce
¼ cup brown sugar
2 teaspoons sesame oil
1 teaspoon olive oil
1 teaspoon chili flakes
2 garlic cloves, minced
1 teaspoon ginger, freshly grated
salt

Prep time: 5 min
Cooking time: 15 min

Preparation:
Mix the brown sugar, soy sauce, sesame oil, ginger, chili flakes and salt in a bowl and set aside.
Pour olive oil into a sauce pan and heat then fry the tofu for about 10 min.
Pour the sauce into the pan and cook for 3-5 min. Serve when the sauce has thickened and the tofu is done.
Nutritional value per serving: 245kcal, 17g protein, 15g carbs (1g fiber, 11g sugar), 15g fat (3g saturated), 34% calcium, 19% iron, 19% magnesium, 11% vitamin B2, 11% vitamin B6.

44.Tuna Melt

Unlike a regular tuna melt that is high in saturated fats and carbs, this one has a moderate amount of carbs and packs the protein-punch of a tuna can, making it an excellent meal that supports lean muscle growth.

Ingredients (2 servings):

1 can of tuna (165g)
2 slices of low-fat mozzarella cheese
2 teaspoons tomato sauce
1 whole wheat English muffin
a sprinkle of oregano

Prep time: 5 min
Cooking time: 3 min

Preparation:
Preheat the oven to 190C fan/ gas 5.
Slice the English muffin then smear each half with the tomato sauce. Top with the tuna, sprinkle with the oregano and place one slice of cheese on top of the tuna. Place the mini-melts in the oven and bake for 2-3 min or until the cheese has melted then divide between 2 plates and serve.
Nutritional value per serving: 255kcal, 31g protein, 14g carbs (2g fiber, 2 g sugar), 6g fat (4g saturated), 29% calcium, 11% iron, 13% magnesium, 10% vitamin B1, 10% vitamin B2, 60% vitamin B3, 23% vitamin B6, 52% vitamin B12.

45.Chicken with Avocado Salad

A meal that provides a great balance of quality protein and healthy fats that will keep you satisfied without overdoing it on the carbs front. Replace the vinegar with lemon juice for a fresher feel.

Ingredients (1 serving):
100g chicken breast

1 teaspoon smoked paprika
2 teaspoons olive oil
For the salad:
½ medium avocado, diced
1 medium tomato, chopped
½ small red onion, thinly sliced
1 tablespoon parsley, roughly chopped
1 teaspoon red wine vinegar

Prep time: 10 min
Cooking time: 10 min

Preparation:
Heat the grill to medium. Rub the chicken with 1 teaspoon olive oil and paprika. Cook for 5 min on each side until it is cooked through and lightly charred. Cut the chicken in thick slices.
Mix the salad ingredients together, season, add the rest of the olive oil and serve with the chicken.
Nutritional value per serving: 346kcal, 26g protein, 14g carbs (6g fiber, 4g sugar), 22g fat (3g saturated), 16% magnesium, 22% vitamin, 44% vitamin C, 18% vitamin E, 38% vitamin K, 12% vitamin B1, 11% vitamin B2, 66% vitamin B3, 19% vitamin B5, 43% vitamin B6, 22% vitamin B9.

SNACKS

1. Cherry Tomatoes with Cottage Cheese

Cut 5 cherry tomatoes in half and smear them with 2 tablespoons goat cheese mixed with fresh dill and a pinch of salt.
Nutritional value: 58kcal, 4g protein, 10g carbs, 30% vitamin A, 40% vitamin C, 20% vitamin K, 10% vitamin B1, 10% vitamin B6, 10% vitamin B9.

2. Avocado on Toast

Toast a small piece of whole wheat bread then cover it with 50g of mashed avocado and sprinkle with salt and pepper.
Nutritional value: 208kcal, 5g protein, 28g carbs (6g fiber, 2g sugar), 9g fat (1g saturated), 13% vitamin K, 13% vitamin B9.

3. Bell Peppers with Cottage Cheese

Cut a small bell pepper in half, deseed it then stuff it with 50g cottage cheese mixed with your choice of seasoning.
Nutritional value: 44kcal, 6g protein, 3g carbs (3g sugar), 49% vitamin C.

4. Rice Cake with Peanut Butter

Spread 1 rice cake with 1 tablespoon creamy peanut butter.
Nutritional value: 129kcal, 5g protein, 10g carbs (1g fiber, 1 g sugar), 8g fat (1g saturated), 10% vitamin B3.

5. Celery Sticks with Goat Cheese and Green Olives

Top 3 medium celery sticks with 3 tablespoons goat cheese and 3 sliced green olives.

Nutritional value: 102kcal, 4g protein, 6g carbs (3g fiber), 6g fat (4g saturated), 12% calcium, 45% vitamin K, 18% vitamin A, 12% vitamin B9.

6. Yogurt with Dried Goji Berries

Mix 150g low-fat yogurt with 10g goji berries.
Nutritional value: 134kcal, 7g protein, 19g carbs (1g fiber, 18% sugar), 4g fat (1g saturated), 27% calcium, 24% iron, 13% vitamin C, 19% vitamin B2, 13% vitamin B12.

7. Apple and Peanut Butter

Slice 1 small apple and spread 1 tablespoon creamy peanut butter on the pieces.
Nutritional value: 189kcal, 4g protein, 28g carbs (5g fiber, 20g sugar), 8g fat (1g saturated), 14% vitamin C, 14% vitamin B3.

8. Greek Yogurt with Strawberries.

Mix 150g Greek Yogurt with 5 medium-sized strawberries cut in half.
Nutritional value: 150kcal, 11g protein, 10g carbs (10g sugar), 8g fat (5g saturated), 10% calcium, 60% vitamin C.

9. Nut Mix

Mix together 10g walnuts, 10g almond and 30g raisins.
Nutritional value: 217kcal, 4g protein, 25g carbs (2g fiber, 17g sugar), 13g fat (1g saturated), 10% magnesium.

10. Ham and Celery Sticks

Wrap 6 medium celery sticks with 3 slices of ham and serve with 1 teaspoon of whole grain mustard.
Nutritional value: 129kcal, 15g protein, 6g carbs (6g fiber), 3g fat, 12% calcium, 24% vitamin A, 12% vitamin C, 90% vitamin K,

18% vitamin B1, 12% vitamin B2, 24% vitamin B3, 15% vitamin B6, 24% vitamin B9.

11. Yogurt with Tropical Fruit

Add 150g Greek Yogurt with ½ cup cut-up kiwi and ¼ cup cut-up mango.
Nutritional value: 210kcal, 12g protein, 25g carbs (2g fiber, 19g sugar), 8g fat (5g saturated), 13% calcium, 11% vitamin A, 155% vitamin C, 46% vitamin K.

12. Blueberry Yogurt

Blend 150g low fat yogurt with ½ cup blueberries.
Nutritional value: 136kcal, 8g protein, 21g carbs (2g fiber, 18g sugar), 3g fat (1g saturated), 27% calcium, 13% vitamin C, 18% vitamin K, 21% vitamin B2, 13% vitamin B12.

13. Cup of Popcorn

Nutritional value: 31kcal, 1g protein, 6g carbs (1g fiber).

14. Roasted Chickpeas

Nutritional value 50g: 96kcal, 4g protein, 13g carbs (4g fiber, 2g sugar), 3g fat.

FAT BURNING CALENDAR

Week 1
Day 1:
Fruit and Nuts Yogurt
Egg Drop Soup with Chicken and Noodles
Mushroom Pilaf with Lemon
Day 2:
Egg and Veggie Breakfast Bakes
Turkey Stir Fry
Stuffed Eggplant
Day 3:
Breakfast Guacamole
Lemmon-rubbed Barbecued Salmon
Orange, Walnut and Blue Cheese Salad
Day 4:
Fitness Smoothie
Chicken and Corn Salad
Veggie Red Curry
Day 5:
Banana Oatmeal Pancakes
Tangy Trout
Stuffed Zucchinis

Day 6:
Tuna on Toast
Garlic Beef
Fruit Salad
Day 7:
Bacon and Brie Omelette with Salad
Rice and Tomato Soup
Smoked Trout with Beetroot, Fennel and Apple Salad

Week 2

Day 1:
Berry Smoothie
Lemon Spaghetti with Broccoli and Tuna
Devilled Mushrooms
Day 2:
Spring Onion and Turkey Wraps
Chicken with Mushrooms
Mexican Rice and Bean Salad
Day 3:
Poached Eggs with Smoked Salmon and Spinach
Bean and Pepper Chili
Thai Vegetable and Coconut Milk Broth
Day 4:
Hummus with Pita Bread and Vegetables
Grilled Fish with Moroccan Spiced Tomatoes
Lentil, Carrot and Orange Soup
Day 5:
Oatmeal with Apples and Raisins
Spicy Seafood Stew
Chickpeas and Spinach Curry
Day 6:
Feta and Semi-dried Tomato Omelette
Spinach and Dates Stuffed Chicken
Roasted Carrots with Pomegranate and Blue Cheese
Day 7:
Fruit and Nuts Yogurt
Prawn Curry
Mexican Rice and Bean Salad

Week 3

Day 1:

Bacon and Brie Omelette with Salad

Bean and Pepper Chili

Tangy Trout

Day 2:

Fitness Smoothie

Garlic Beef

Stuffed Eggplant

Day 3:

Breakfast Guacamole

Turkey Stir Fry

Fruit Salad

Day 4:

Egg and Veggie Breakfast Bakes

Lemon-rubbed Barbecued Salmon

Veggie Red Curry

Day 5:

Banana Oatmeal Pancakes

Egg Drop Soup with Chicken and Noodles

Smoked Trout with Beetroot, Fennel and Apple Salad

Day 6:

Tuna on Toast

Rice and Tomato Soup

Stuffed Zucchinis

Day 7:

Berry Smoothie

Chicken and Corn Salad

Orange, Walnut and Blue Cheese Dressing

Week 4

Day 1:
Oatmeal with Apples and Raisins
Lemon Spaghetti with Broccoli and Tuna
Lentil, Carrot and Orange Soup
Day 2:
Poached Eggs with Smoked Salmon and Spinach
Chicken with Mushrooms
Chickpeas and Spinach Curry
Day 3:
Spring Onion and Turkey Wraps
Spicy seafood Stew
Roasted Carrots with Pomegranate and Blue Cheese
Day 4:
Feta and Semi-dried Tomato Omelette
Bean and Pepper Chili
Fruit Salad
Day 5:
Hummus with Pita Bread and Vegetables
Prawn Curry
Mexican Rice and Bean Salad
Day 6:
Fruit and Nuts Yogurt
Spinach and Dates Stuffed Chicken
Thai Vegetable and Coconut Broth
Day 7:
Breakfast Guacamole
Tangy trout
Stuffed Eggplant

2 extra days for a full month:

Day 1:

Fitness Smoothie
Chicken and Corn Salad
Orange, Walnut and Blue Cheese Salad
Day 2:
Tuna on Toast
Turkey Stir Fry
Veggie Red Curry

HIGH PERFORMANCE MEAL RECIPES TO BURN FAT

BREAKFAST
1. Feta and Semi-dried Tomato Omelette

A really quick, simple, low calorie recipe that will give your day the kick start it deserves. For an extra pinch of flavor, use tomatoes that have been preserved in a mixture of olive oil and Italian herbs.

Ingredients (1 serving):
2 eggs, lightly beaten
25g feta cheese, crumbled
4 semi-dried tomatoes, roughly chopped
1 teaspoon olive oil
mixed salad leaves, for serving

Prep time: 5 min
Cooking time: 5 min

Preparation:
Heat the oil in a small, non-stick frying pan, then add the eggs and cook, swirling them with a wooden spoon. When the eggs are a bit runny in the middle, add the tomatoes and feta, then fold the omelet in half. Cook for 1 min, then slide it onto a plate and serve with a mix of leaf salad.
Nutritional value per serving: 300kcal, 18g protein, 20g fat (7 saturated), 5g carbs (1g fiber, 4g sugar), 1.8g salt, 15% calcium, 22% vitamin D, 20% vitamin A, 15% vitamin C, 25% vitamin B12.

2. Oatmeal with Apples and Raisins

A warm, filling, calcium rich breakfast that is easy on the stomach and perfect as a pre-workout meal, due to its high carb content. Sprinkle with some cinnamon for a sweet, woody fragrance.

Ingredients (2 servings):
50g oats
250ml low-fat milk
2 apples, peeled and diced
50g raisins
½ tablespoon honey

Prep time: 5min
Cooking time: 10 min

Preparation:
Bring the milk to a boil in a saucepan over medium heat and stir with the oats for 3 minutes. When the concoction becomes creamy, add the apples and the raisins and boil for another 2min. Ladle the mix into 2 bowls, add the honey and serve immediately.

Nutritional value per serving: 256kcal, 9g protein, 2g fat (1g saturated), 47g carbs (4g fiber, 34g sugar), 17% calcium, 11% iron, 17% magnesium.

3. Hummus with Pita Bread and Vegetables

This is a simple and nutritious breakfast that you can quickly assemble in the morning and pack to work. The hummus stays in the fridge and the vegetables can be stuffed into the pita bread, making an easy to grab sandwich.

Ingredients (2 servings):
1 200g can of chickpeas, drained
1 clove of garlic, crushed
25g of tahini
¼ teaspoon cumin
lemon juice, squeezed from ¼ lemon
salt, pepper
3 tablespoons water
2 whole wheat pita bread
200g vegetable mix (carrots, celery, cucumber)

Prep time: 15 min
No cooking

Preparation:
Combine chickpeas, garlic, tahini, cumin, lemon juice, salt, pepper and water in a food processor and pulse several times until the mix becomes creamy.
Serve with toasted pita bread and vegetable mix.
Nutritional value per serving: 239kcal, 9g protein, 9g fat (1g saturated), 28g carbs (6g fiber, 4g sugar), 1,1g salt, 27% iron, 23% magnesium, 14% vitamin B1.

4. Spring Onion and Turkey Wraps

What better way to use leftover turkey bits, than to make a quick delicious tortilla sandwich? Give yourself a treat that is high in protein, low in saturated fat and flavored with the zesty taste of basil.

Ingredients (2 servings):
130g cooked turkey (boiled or roasted), shredded
3 spring onions, shredded
1 chunk of cucumber, shredded
2 curly lettuce leaves
1 tablespoons light mayonnaise
1 tablespoon pesto
2 whole wheat flour tortillas

Prep time: 5mins
No cooking
Preparation:
Mix together the pesto and mayonnaise. Divide the turkey, spring onions, cucumber and lettuce leaves between the 2 tortillas. Drizzle over the pesto dressing, wrap everything up and serve.
Nutritional value per serving: 267kcal, 24g protein, 9g fat (2g saturated), 25g carbs (2g fiber, 3g sugar), 1.6g salt, 34% vitamin B3, 27% vitamin B6.

5. Berry Smoothie

What better way to get half a day's worth of calcium than with this creamy yogurt based meal? Add some fibers and make it even more nutritional, by saving half the berries from the blender and tipping them over when the smoothie is done.

Ingredients (2 servings):
450g frozen berries
450g low fat yogurt
100ml low fat milk
25g porridge oats
1 teaspoon honey (optional)

Prep time: 10 min
No cooking

Preparation:
Mix the berries, yogurt and milk in a food processor until smooth. Then add and stir the porridge oats and pour into 2 glasses. Serve with a bit of honey.
Nutritional value per serving: 234kcal, 16g protein, 2g fat (2g saturated), 36g carbs (14g sugar), 45% calcium, 11% magnesium, 18% vitamin B2, 21% vitamin B12.

6. Poached Eggs with Smoked Salmon and Spinach

A filling, high-protein breakfast that will give your day a very satisfying start. You will have no problem reaching your daily requirement of vitamin A and your heart will thank you for the hearty amount of omega-3 fatty acids.

Ingredients (1 serving):
2 eggs
100g spinach, chopped
50g smoked salmon
1 tablespoon white vinegar
a little butter for spreading
1 piece of whole wheat bread, toasted

Prep time: 5 min
Cooking time: 20 min

Preparation:
Heat a non-stick frying pan, add the spinach and stir for 2 min. In order to poach the eggs, bring a pan of water to the boiling point, add the vinegar and then lower the heat so that the water is simmering. Stir the water until you have a slight whirlpool then slide the eggs one by one. Cook each for about 4 minutes then remove the egg with a slotted spoon.
Butter the piece of toast then put the spinach on it, the smoked salmon and the eggs. Season as needed and serve.
Nutritional value per serving: 349kcal, 31g protein, 19g fat (6g saturated), 13g carbs (4g fiber, 2g sugar), 3.6g salt, 23% iron, 23% magnesium, 197% vitamin A, 46% vitamin C, 21% vitamin D, 15% vitamin B6, 18% vitamin B12.

7. Bacon and Brie Omelette with Salad

A tasty omelette for those who prefer starting the day with a healthy filling of eggs and protein. Cut the omelette into wedges for a frittata look and savor with a salad instead of bread to cut back on the calories.

Ingredients (2 servings):
3 eggs, lightly beaten
100g smoked lardoons
50g brie, sliced
a small bunch of chives, chopped
1 tablespoon olive oil
½ teaspoon red wine vinegar
½ teaspoon Dijon mustard
½ cucumber, halved and deseeded
100g radishes, quartered

Prep time: 5 min
Cooking time 15 min

Preparation:
Heat 1 teaspoon in a small pan, add the lardoons and fry until crisp, then take it out of the pan and let it drain on kitchen paper.
Heat 1 teaspoon of the oil in a non-stick frying pan, then mix together the lardoons, eggs and some ground pepper. Pour into the frying pan and cook over low heat until it is almost done, then add the Brie and grill until it is set and golden.
Mix the remaining olive oil, vinegar, seasoning and mustard in a bowl and toss the radishes and cucumber. Serve alongside the omelette.

Nutritional value per serving: 395kcal, 25g protein, 31g fat (12g saturated), 3g carbs (2g fiber, 3g sugar), 2.2g salt, 10% vitamin A, 13% vitamin C, 15% vitamin D, 13% vitamin B12.

8. Fitness smoothie

A dairy-free vegan smoothie with pomegranate juice that will energize you for work or sustain your workout. You can add a tablespoon of ground flaxseeds for another 2g of fiber at the low cost of an extra 37kcal.

Ingredients (1 serving):
125ml soya milk
150ml pomegranate juice
30g tofu
1 large banana, cut into chunks
1 teaspoon honey
1 tablespoon almond
2 ice cubes

Prep time: 5 min
No cooking

Preparation:
Blend the soya milk and pomegranate juice with 2 ice cubes until the ice has broken down.
Add the banana, honey and tofu and blend until smooth, then pour the mix into a glass and sprinkle it with the flaked almonds.
Nutritional value per serving: 366kcal, 10g protein, 12g fat (1g saturated), 55g carbs (4g fiber, 50g sugar), 13% calcium, 11% iron, 15% magnesium, 14% vitamin C, 25% vitamin B6.

9. Tuna on Toast

A really quick, low calorie recipe that delivers a high amount of neuron protective B12. If you want an energy boost, spread the paste on a piece of whole wheat bread at about 120kcal per piece and serve with the bell pepper on the side.

Ingredients (4 servings):

2 cans of tuna in water (185g), half drained

3 hard-boiled eggs

1 spring onion, finely chopped

5 small pickles, diced

salt, pepper

4 bell peppers, halved, with the seeds cleaned

Prep time: 5 min

Cooking time: 10 min

Preparation:

Combine the tuna, eggs, spring onion, pickles and seasoning in a food processor and mix until smooth.

Fill the halves of the bell peppers with the composition and serve.

Nutritional value per serving: 240kcal, 23g protein, 8g fat (2g saturated), 4g carbs (1g fiber, 2g sugar), 14% magnesium, 47% vitamin A, 28% vitamin B6, 142% vitamin B12,.

10. Banana Oatmeal Pancakes

Enjoy this healthier version of pancakes that replaces plain flower with rolled oats. The banana makes for a subtle sugar substitute, but you can also spread 1 teaspoon of honey (23kcal per teaspoon) if you feel like it.

Ingredients (8 pancakes):
50g rolled oats
4 eggs, lightly beaten
2 bananas, cut into chunks
½ teaspoon cinnamon
1 teaspoon olive oil for each pancake

Prep time: 5 min
Cooking time: 30 min

Preparation:
Combine all the ingredients in a food processor. Heat a non-stick frying pan, add a teaspoon of oil and drop ¼ cup of mix into the pan. Cook on each size until the pancake become lightly brown.
Nutritional value per pancake: 135kcal, 4g protein, 13g fat (3g saturated), 10g carbs (1g fiber, 3g sugar).

11. Breakfast Guacamole

You can't miss with a meal that contains avocado. High in healthy fats and fiber, with a smooth texture and a flavor richly enhanced by a bit of lemon juice, this breakfast guacamole will energize you till lunch.

Ingredients (2 servings):
1 ripe avocado
1 large tomato, roughly chopped
1 spring onion, finely chopped
1 clove of garlic crushed
lemon juice, from ½ lemon
salt
ground black pepper
2 slices of whole wheat bread, toasted

Prep time: 5 min
No cooking

Preparation:
Slice the avocado in half, lengthwise, then scoop out the pulp with a spoon and put it into a large bowl. Mash it up with a fork. Pour the lemon juice over the pulp and add the chopped tomato, the spring onion and garlic. Season with salt and lots of black pepper. Mix it around, spread it on a piece of toast and serve immediately.

Nutritional value per serving: 280kcal, 9g protein, 13g fat (2g saturated), 30g carbs (9g fiber, 5g sugar), 10% iron, 17% magnesium, 14% vitamin A, 29% vitamin C, 17% vitamin B6.

12. Egg and Veggies Breakfast Bakes

An inventive, easy to make breakfast that bakes an egg instead of frying it, saving you a substantial amount of saturated fats. The eggs make it filling, while the veggies are not only tasty but also loaded with vitamin A and C.

Ingredients (1 serving):
2 large field mushrooms
2 medium-sized tomatoes, halved
100g spinach
2 eggs
1 garlic clove, thinly sliced
1 teaspoon olive oil

Prep time: 5 min
Cooking time: 30 min

Preparation:
Heat the oven to 200C fan/gas 6. Put in the tomatoes and mushrooms into an ovenproof dish. Add the garlic, drizzle the oil and seasoning and then bake for 10 min.
Put the spinach in a large pan then pour over a kettle of boiling water to wilt it. Squeeze out the excess water and then add the spinach to the dish. Make a little gap between the veggies and crack the eggs into the dish. Cook for another 10 min in the oven until the eggs are done.
Nutritional value per serving: 254kcal, 18g protein, 16g fat (4g saturated), 16g carbs (6g fiber, 10g sugar), 31% iron, 17% calcium, 29% magnesium, 238% vitamin A, 11% vitamin D, 102% vitamin C, 18% vitamin B1, 51% vitamin B2, 20% vitamin B3, 29% vitamin B6, 22% vitamin B12.

13. Fruit and Nuts Yogurt

A great alternative to cereal, this high-carb breakfast will keep you full till lunch and give you the energy start you require to tackle your tasks. The mix of nuts delivers a substantial amount of healthy fats, while the yogurt makes sure that you get half a day's worth of calcium.

Ingredients (1 serving):
1 medium-sized banana, sliced
100g blueberries (fresh or frozen and defrosted)
20g walnuts
20g hazelnuts
10g raisins
200g fat free yogurt

Prep time: 5 min
No cooking

Preparation:
Mix the fruit with the nuts, layer up in a bowl with yogurt and serve.
Nutritional value per serving: 450kcal, 13g protein, 25g fat (2g saturated), 54g carbs (9g fiber, 32g sugar), 44% calcium, 16% magnesium, 30% vitamin C, 36% vitamin B6.

LUNCH

14. Egg Drop Soup with Chicken and Noodles

A quick and easy to make dish, perfect for a midday meal. The noodles contain enough energy boosting carbs that will sustain your throughout the day and the meat is loaded with vitamin B.

Ingredients (2 servings):
1 skinless, boneless chicken breasts, diced
1 egg, beaten
0.6l chicken soup
1 spring onion, finely chopped
70g whole wheat noodles
70g frozen sweet corn, or baby corn, halved lengthways
lemon juice
¼ teaspoon sherry vinegar

Prep time: 10 min
Cooking time: 15 min

Preparation:
Place the chicken and the soup in a large pan and bring to a simmer for 5 min. The noodles are to be cooked following the instructions on the pack.
Add the corn and boil for 2 min. Stir the broth and while it is still churning, hold a fork over the pan and pour the eggs over the prongs in a slow stream. Stir again in the same direction and then take it off the heat. Add the lemon juice and the vinegar.

Drain the noodles and divide them between 2 bowls. Pour the broth, scatter with the chopped onions and serve.
Nutritional value per serving: 273kcal, 26g protein, 6g fat (1g saturated), 30g carbs (3g fiber, 2g sugar), 1g salt, 96% vitamin B3, 42% vitamin B6.

15. Chicken and Corn Salad

 A paprika-spiced chicken, served with grilled sweet corn and fresh, crisp lettuce, makes for a healthy, speedy salad, with copious amounts of vitamin B. The garlic based dressing tops an already tasty meal.

Ingredients (2 servings):
2 small skinless chicken breasts
1 corn cob
2 little gem lettuces, quartered lengthways
½ cucumber, diced
1 garlic cloves, crushed
1 tablespoon olive oil
1 teaspoon paprika
lemon juice, from half a lemon

salad dressing (2 servings):
1 clove garlic, crushed
75ml curd milk
1 tablespoon white wine vinegar

Prep time: 20 min
Cooking time: 20 min
Preparation:

Cut the chicken breasts lengthways in half so you are left with 4 chicken strips. Mix the paprika, garlic, 1 teaspoon oil and lemon juice with some seasoning and marinate the chicken for at least 20 min.

Heat a pan, add the remaining oil and cook the chicken for 3-4 min on each side until it is cooked through. Brush over the remaining oil and griddle the corn for about 5 min or until lightly charred. Make sure to cook evenly. Remove the corn cobs and cut off the kernels.

Combine the ingredients for the dressing.

Mix the cucumber and lettuce, put the chicken and corn on top and drizzle the dressing.

Nutritional value per serving : 253kcal, 29g protein, 8g fat (1g saturated), 14g carbs (3g fiber, 6g sugar), 20% iron, 40% magnesium, 96% vitamin B3, 72% vitamin B6.

16. Lemon Spaghetti with Broccoli and Tuna

15 minutes is all you need to whip up this zesty fish pasta that packs a significant energy punch. The mix of spaghetti, tuna and vegetable make this an all-round nutritious dish.

Ingredients (2 servings):
180g whole wheat spaghetti
100g can tuna in oil, drained
125g broccoli, cut into florets
40g pitted green olives, quartered
1 tablespoon capers, drained
juice and zest from ½ lemon
1 teaspoon olive oil, plus extra for drizzling

Prep time: 5 min

Cooking time: 10 min

Preparation:
Boil the spaghetti according to the instructions on the pack. 6 min in, add the broccoli and boil for 4 min or more until both are tender.
Mix the olives, shallots, capers, tuna, lemon zest and juice in a big bowl. Drain the pasta and broccoli, add to the bowl, mix well with the olive oil and black pepper and serve.
Nutritional value per serving: 440kcal, 23g protein, 11g fat (2g saturated), 62g carbs (5g fiber, 4g sugar), 1.4g salt, 12% iron, 20% magnesium, 25% vitamin A, 50% vitamin B3, 25% vitamin B6, 90% vitamin B12.

17. Lemon-rubbed Barbecued Salmon

Rich in healthy fats, protein and B vitamins, salmon is a fish that definitely deserves a spot on you plate. Serve with a simple mix of tomato and green salad to savor the fine taste of this lemony meal.

Ingredients (2 servings):
2*150g boneless salmon fillets
juice and zest ½ lemon
10g fresh tarragon, finely chopped
1 garlic clove, finely chopped
1 tablespoon oil

Prep time: 5 min
Cooking time: 10 min

Preparation:

Stir the lemon zest and juice, garlic, tarragon and olive oil in a dish, season with salt and pepper and then add the salmon fillets. Rub the mixture on the fish, cover and set aside for 10 min.

Heat the grill to high, remove the salmon fillets from the marinade, put them on a baking shit and grill for 7-10 min. Served when the salmon is just cooked through.

Nutritional value per serving: 322kcal, 31g protein, 22g fat (4g saturated), 1g carbs, 12% vitamin B2, 30% vitamin B1, 60% vitamin B3, 45% vitamin B6, 79% vitamin B12.

18. Rice and Tomato Soup

A hearty main course, the rice and tomato soup is a great way to take advantage of the fresh and savory tomatoes available in summer. You can also serve it cold, for a refreshing effect.

Ingredients (2 servings):
70g brown rice
200g tomatoes, chopped
1 teaspoon tomato puree
1 spring onion, finely chopped
1 small carrot, finely chopped
½ celery stick, finely chopped
½ l vegetable stock made with 1 cube
1 teaspoon golden caster sugar
1 teaspoon vinegar
a few parsley leaves, chopped
a few drops of pesto, to serve (optional)

Prep time: 10 min

Cooking time: 35 min

Preparation:
Heat the oil in a large pan, add the carrot, celery and onion and cook on medium heat until softened. Add the vinegar and sugar, cook for 1 min and then stir through the tomato puree. Add the tomatoes, the vegetable stock and the brown rise, cover and simmer for 10 min.
Divide into 2 bowls, and sprinkle some parsley, season. Add pesto if wanted.
Nutritional value per serving: 213kcal, 6g protein, 3g fat (1g saturated), 39g carbs (4g fiber, 13g sugar), 1.6g salt, 16% vitamin A, 22% vitamin C.

19. Spinach and Dates Stuffed Chicken

High in protein, with a balanced amount of carbs and lots of vitamins, this healthy meal covers pretty much everything, from nutrients to taste. The date and spinach stuffing add a welcomed sweetness.

Ingredients (2 servings):
2 boneless and skinless chicken breasts
100g spinach, chopped
1 small onion, finely chopped
1 garlic clove, finely chopped
4 dates, finely chopped
1 tablespoon pomegranate juice or honey
1 teaspoon cumin
1 tablespoon olive oil
100g frozen green beans

Prep time: 10 min
Cooking time: 15 min.

Preparation:
Heat the oven to 200C fan/gas 6. Heat the oil in a non-stick pan, add the onion, garlic and a dash of salt and cook for 5 min before adding the dates, spinach and ½ of the cumin. Cook for another 1-2 min.

Cut the chicken breasts in half, lengthways, and leave a part intact so as to be able to open them like a book. Stuff the chicken breasts and put them in an oven pan, add the rest of the cumin and seasoning, sprinkle with the honey or pomegranate juice and bake for 20 min. Serve with the frozen green peas, slightly steamed.

Nutritional value per serving: 257kcal, 36g protein, 4g fat (1g saturated), 21g carbs (3g fiber), 17% iron, 23% magnesium, 97% vitamin A, 36% vitamin C, 96% vitamin B3, 49% vitamin B6.

20. Bean and Pepper Chili

A healthy vegetarian midday meal with a spicy kick, this dish is a great way of getting 1/2 – 1/3 of your daily required amount of fiber. You can serve topped on a small portion of boiled brown rice with around 170kcal added to your meal.

Ingredients (2 servings):
170g peppers, deseeded and sliced
200g can kidney beans in chili sauce
200g can black beans, drained
200g tomatoes, chopped
1 small onion, chopped

1 teaspoon cumin
1 teaspoon chili powder
1 teaspoon sweet smoked paprika
1 teaspoon olive oil

Prep time: 15 min
Cooking time: 30 min

Preparation:
Heat the oil in a large pan, add the onion and pepper and cook for 8-10 min until softened. Add the spices and cook for 1 min. Tip the beans and tomatoes, bring to a boil and simmer for 15 min. When the chili has thickened season and serve.
Nutritional value per serving: 183kcal, 11g protein, 5g fat (1g saturated), 26g carbs (12g fiber, 12g sugar), 16% iron, 14% magnesium, 16% vitamin A, 22% vitamin C, 14% vitamin B1.

21. Garlic Beef

Enjoy a quickly made beef steak that is not only high in protein and low in fat and carbs, but also loaded with vitamin B. Pair it with some cherry tomatoes for a filling and refreshing meal.

Ingredients (2 servings):
300g well-trimmed beef skirt
3 garlic cloves
2 tablespoons red wine vinegar
1 teaspoon black peppercorn
200g cherry tomatoes, halved with a splash of vinegar

Prep time: 10 min

Cooking time: 15min

Preparation:
Crush the peppercorns and garlic with a pinch of salt in a pestle and mortar until you have a slightly smooth paste, then stir in the vinegar. Sit the beef in dish, then rub the paste all over. Leave in the fridge for 2 hours.

Place a griddle pan over a very hot heat. Rub the marinade off the meat, add more salt. Cook the meat for about 5 min until charred on each side (make sure the cut is not too thick). Lift the meat onto a chopping board, then rest for 5 min before carving it into slices. Serve with cherry tomatoes.

Nutritional value per serving: 223kcal, 34g protein, 6g fats, 7g carbs (1g fiber, 3g sugar), 22% iron, 16% vitamin A, 22% vitamin C, 27% vitamin B2, 42% vitamin B3, 30% vitamin B6, 64% vitamin B12.

22. Grilled Fish with Moroccan Spiced Tomatoes

A sea bream based meal makes for an excellent source of protein. The South African sauce with its aromatic spices compliments its taste and it also goes well with sardines and sea bass.

Ingredients (2 servings):
2*140g skinless sea bream fillets
3 large tomatoes
1 ½ large red peppers, deseeded and halved
2 garlic cloves, crushed
20ml olive oil
1 teaspoon cumin

1 teaspoon ground paprika
1/8 teaspoon black pepper
a pinch of cayenne
small bunch parsley, roughly chopped
small bunch coriander, roughly chopped

Prep time: 30 min
Cooking time: 15 min

Preparation:
Heat the grill to high, place the peppers skin side up on a
baking tray and place under the grill until black and blistered.
Place in a bowl covered tightly and let them cool. When they
are cool, remove the burnt skins then cut them into small
pieces.
Skin the tomatoes, then cut into quarters, discard the seeds
and dice.
Heat the oil in a large pan, add the garlic, the ground pepper
and the spices and cook for 2 min. Add the peppers and
tomatoes and cook over medium heat until the tomatoes are
very soft. Smash the soft tomatoes and continue cooking until
the liquid is reduced to sauce.
Heat the grill to high, place the fish on a baking tray lined with
lightly oiled foil. Season and grill for 4-5 min until cooked
through. Divide the sauce between plates place the fish on top
and serve with the chopped herbs.
 Nutritional value per serving: 308kcal, 25g protein, 18g fat (2g
saturated), 16g carbs (4g fiber, 12 g sugar), 23% magnesium,
45% vitamin A, 55% vitamin C, 12% vitamin B1, 12% vitamin
B2, 14% vitamin B3, 34% vitamin B6.

23.Prawn Curry

You only need 20 min to make this delicious, curry flavored seafood dish. The creamy, aromatic cherry sauce goes very well with a serving of boiled brown rice at about 175kcal per serving.

Ingredients (2 servings):
200g raw frozen prawns
200g chopped tomatoes
25g sachet coconut cream
1 small onion, chopped
1 teaspoon Thai red curry paste
½ teaspoon fresh ginger root
1 teaspoon olive oil
coriander, chopped

Prep time: 5 min
Cooking time: 15 min

Preparation:
Heat the oil in a saucepan. Tip in the onion and ginger and cook for a few minutes until softened. Add the curry paste, stir and cook for 1 more min. Pour over the tomatoes and coconut cream, bring to boil and leave to simmer for 5 min, adding a little boiling water if the concoction gets too thick.
Add the prawns and cook for another 5-10 min. Sprinkle with the chopped coriander and serve.
Nutritional value per serving: 180kcal, 20g protein, 9g fat (4g saturated), 6g carbs (1g fiber, 5g sugar), 1g salt, 18% iron, 10% magnesium, 20% vitamin A, 26% vitamin C, 13% vitamin B3, 25% vitamin B12.

24. Chicken with Mushrooms

A healthy dish, this chicken casserole has a high amount of protein that will keep you full until dinner. The chicken thighs add extra flavor and juiciness, while the mushrooms are responsible for the tangy feel of this low calories midday meal.

Ingredients (2 servings):
250g boneless, skinless chicken thighs
125ml chicken stock
25g frozen peas
150g mushrooms
25g cubetti di pancetta
1 large shallot, chopped
1 tablespoon olive oil
1 teaspoon white wine vinegar
flour, for dusting
small handful parsley, finely chopped

Prep time: 15 min
Cooking time: 25 min

Preparation:
Heat 1 teaspoon of oil in a non-stick frying pan, season and dust the chicken with the flour. Brown on all sides then remove the chicken and fry the pancetta and mushrooms until softened.
And the rest of the olive oil and cook the shallots for 5 min. Add the stock, the vinegar and bubble for 1-2 min. Return the chicken, pancetta and mushrooms to the pan and cook for 15 min. Add the peas and parsley, cook for 2 more minutes, then serve.

Nutritional value per serving: 260kcal, 32g protein, 13g fat (3g saturated), 4g carbs (3g fiber, 1 g sugar), 1g salt, 21% iron, 39% vitamin D, 12% vitamin B2, 34% vitamin B3, 17% vitamin B6.

25. Turkey Stir Fry

High in protein, quickly made and flavorsome, this dish is a perfect, spicy lunch. Its carbs content will load you with energy so it can also be an ideal pre-workout meal.

Ingredients (2 servings):
200g turkey breast steaks, cut into strips (remove fat)
150g rice noodles
170g green beans, halved
1 garlic clove, sliced
1 small red onion, sliced
½ red chili, finely chopped
juice from ½ lime
½ teaspoon olive oil
½ teaspoon chili powder
1 teaspoon fish sauce
Mint, roughly chopped
Coriander, roughly chopped

Prep time: 10 min
Cooking time: 15 min

Preparation:
Cook the noodles following the instructions on the pack. Heat the oil in a non-stick pan and fry the turkey over a high heat for 2 min. Add the onion, garlic and beans and cook for another 5 min.

Tip over the lime juice, fresh chili, chili powder and fish sauce, stir and cook for 3 min. Stir in the noodles and herbs according to taste and serve.

Nutritional value per serving: 425kcal, 32g protein, 3g fat (1g saturated), 71g carbs (4g fiber, 4g sugar), 1 g salt, 12% iron, 10% magnesium, 12% vitamin A, 36% vitamin C, 13% vitamin B1, 24% vitamin B2.

26. Tangy Trout

Try this easy, healthy trout recipe for a light summer meal. A great source of vitamin B12, this lemony white fish can be served with a side of green salad sprinkled with sea salt and a bit of lemon juice for an extra zesty feel.

Ingredients (2 servings):
2 trout fillets
15g pine nuts, toasted and roughly chopped
25g breadcrumbs
1 teaspoon soft butter
1 teaspoon olive oil
juice and zest from ½ lemon
1 small bunch of parsley, chopped

Prep time: 10 min
Cooking time: 5 min

Preparation:
Heat the grill to high. Lay the fillets, skin side down on an oiled baking tray.
 Mix the breadcrumbs, lemon juice and zest, butter, parsley and half the pine nuts. Scatter the composition in a thin layer

over the fillets, drizzle with the oil and place under the grill for 5 min. Sprinkle over the rest of the pine nuts and serve with steamed cauliflower or green beans.

Nutritional value per serving: 298kcal, 30g protein, 16g fat (4g saturated), 10g carbs (1g fiber, 1g sugar), 11% magnesium, 14% vitamin B1, 41% vitamin B3, 25% vitamin B6, 150% vitamin B12.

27. Spicy Seafood Stew

Treat your senses to this spicy mix of prawns, clams and white fish that delivers a hearty amount of protein and covers most of the B vitamins. Make sure to use fresh seafood to maximize the savory taste of this one-pot casserole.

Ingredients (2 servings):
100g large peeled raw prawns
150g clams
150g white fish fillets (cut into 3 cm pieces)
250g small new potatoes, halved and boiled
130g chopped tomatoes
350ml chicken stock
1 small onion, chopped
2 garlic cloves, chopped
1 dried ancho chili
juice from 1 lime
½ teaspoon smoked hot paprika
½ teaspoon ground cumin
1 teaspoon olive oil
lime wedges for serving (optional)

Prep time: 15 min

Cooking time: 30 min

Preparation:
Toast the chilies in a hot, dry frying pan until they puff up a bit, then remove, deseed and stem them. Soak in boiling water for 15 min.
Heat the olive oil in a large pan, add the onion, garlic and season and cook until softened. Add the paprika, chili, cumin, tomatoes and stock and sauté for 5 min, then puree in a blender until smooth. Pour back into the pan and bring to the boiling point. Let it simmer for 10 min. Add the prawns, fish fillets, clams and potatoes, place a lid on top of the pan and cook for 5 min over a medium-high heat. Serve with lime wedges if you like.
Nutritional value per serving: 347kcal, 44g protein, 6g fat (1 g saturated), 28g carbs (4g fiber, 7g sugar), 1.1g salt, 18% magnesium, 12% vitamin A, 40% vitamin C, 16% vitamin B1, 10% vitamin B2, 23% vitamin B3, 26% vitamin B6, 62% vitamin B12.

DINNER

28.Stuffed Eggplant

A savory veggie meal, with a crisp cheese and breadcrumbs topping, that is light and perfect for dinner. Forget stuffed peppers and try this flavored eggplant instead.

Ingredients (2 serving):
1 eggplant
60g vegetarian mozzarella, torn into pieces
1 small onion, finely chopped
2 garlic cloves, finely chopped
1 tablespoon olive oil, plus extra for drizzling
2 garlic cloves, finely chopped
6 cherry tomatoes, cut in half
a handful of basil leaves, chopped
a few fresh whole eat breadcrumbs

Prep time: 15 min
Cooking time: 40 min

Preparation:
Heat the oven to 200C fan/gas 7. Slash the eggplant lengthways in half (you can leave the stem intact or remove it). Cut a border inside the eggplant about 1 cm thick. Using a teaspoon, scoop out the eggplant flesh until you are left with 2 shells. Chop the flesh then place it aside. Brush the shells with a little oil, season and place them in a baking dish. Cover it with a foil and bake for 20 min.
Add the remaining oil to a non-stick frying pan. Add the onion and cook until it is soft, then tip in the chopped eggplant flesh

and cook through. Add the garlic and tomatoes and cook for another 3 min.

When the eggplant shells are tender, remove them from the oven, stuff them, sprinkle some breadcrumbs and drizzle with a little bit of oil. Reduce the heat in the oven to 180C fan/ gas 6. Bake for 15-20 min, until the cheese has melted and the breadcrumbs are golden. Serve with a green salad.

Nutritional value per serving: 266kcal, 9g protein, 20g fat (6g saturated), 14g carbs (5g fiber, 7g sugar), 1g salt, 15% vitamin A, 19% calcium.

29. Orange, Walnut and Blue Cheese Salad

Try this salty and sweet salad with crumbled blue cheese and chopped walnuts for a light supper. This, high in healthy fats and vitamin C, no cook recipe takes only 10 min to make and is a great way to end a busy day.

Ingredients (2 servings):
1*100g bag of bag of mixed salad (spinach, rocket and watercress)
1 large orange
40g walnuts, roughly chopped
70g blue cheese, crumbled
1 teaspoon walnut oil

Prep time: 10 min
No cooking

Preparation:
Empty the salad bag into a bowl. Peel the oranges and cut the segments from the pith over a small bowl to catch the juice.

Whisk the walnut oil into the orange juice then pour over the salad leaves. Toss the salad, scatter over the orange segments, blue cheese and walnuts and serve.

Nutritional value per serving: 356kcal, 14g protein, 30g fat (10g saturated), 8g carbs (3g fiber, 8g sugar), 19% calcium, 10% magnesium, 20% vitamin A, 103% vitamin C, 10% vitamin B1.

30. Mexican Rice and Bean Salad

A low fat spicy meal with Latin American flavors, the Mexican rice and bean salad is packed with vegetables and makes for a filling supper. Tweak it a little and use a can of mixed beans for a more colorful plate.

Ingredients (2 servings):
90g brown rice
200g can black bean salad, drained
½ ripe avocado, chopped
2 spring onions, chopped
½ red pepper, deseeded and chopped
Juice from ½ lime
1 teaspoon Cajun spice mix
small bunch of coriander, chopped

Prep time: 15 min
Cooking time: 20 min

Preparation:
Cook the rice following the instructions on the pack. Drain then cool under running water until cold. Stir in the beans, pepper, onions and avocado.

Mix the lime juice with black pepper and the Cajun spices then pour over the rice. Add the coriander and serve.
Nutritional value per serving: 326kcal, 11g protein, 10g fat (2g saturated), 44g carbs (6g fiber, 4g sugar), 10% iron, 15% magnesium, 11% vitamin B1, 13% vitamin B6.

31. Chickpeas and Spinach Curry

Whip up this warming meal for a great night in. High in vitamin A and protein, this veggie dish can be served with a bit of Naan. Watch out for the extra calories though, one piece of Naan bread contains about 140kcal.

Ingredients (2 servings):
1*400g can chickpeas, drained
200g cherry tomatoes
130g baby spinach leaves
1 tablespoon curry paste
1 small onion, chopped
lemon juice

Prep time: 5 min
Cooking time: 15 min

Preparation:
Heat the curry paste in a non-stick frying pan. When it starts to split, add the onion and cook for 2 min until it softens. Tip in the tomatoes and bubble until the sauce has reduced.
Add the chickpeas and some seasoning and cook for an extra minute. Take off the heat, then tip the spinach (the heat of the pan will wilt the leaves). Season, add the lemon juice and serve.

Nutritional value per serving: 203kcal, 9g protein, 4g fat, 28g carbs (6g fiber, 5g sugar), 1.5g salt, 25% iron, 29% magnesium, 129% vitamin A, 61% vitamin C, 58% vitamin B6.

32. Thai Vegetable and Coconut Milk Broth

A serving of egg noodles topped with a delicious vegetable broth gives you a delectable and quick taste of Thai. If you prefer a thicker broth, use less vegetable stock, according to taste.

Ingredients (2 servings):
200ml can half-fat coconut milk
500ml vegetable stock
90g egg noodles
1 carrot, cut into matchsticks
¼ head Chinese leaf, sliced
75g beansprouts
3 cherry tomatoes, halved
2 small spring onions, halved and sliced lengthways
juice form ½ lime
1 ½ teaspoons Thai red curry paste
1 teaspoon brown sugar
1 teaspoon olive oil
handful coriander, roughly chopped

Prep time: 15 min
Cooking time 10 min

Preparation:

Heat the oil in a wok then add the curry paste and fry for 1 min until fragrant. Add the vegetable stock, brown sugar and coconut milk and simmer for 3 min.
Tip in the noodles, carrots and Chinese leaf and simmer until tender. Add the beansprouts and tomatoes, lime juice to taste and some extra seasoning. Spoon into bowls and sprinkle with coriander and spring onions.
Nutritional value: 338kcal, 10g protein, 14g fat (7g saturated), 46g carbs (5g fiber, 12g sugar), 1.2g salt, 14% iron, 16% magnesium, 10% vitamin B3.

33. Stuffed Zucchinis

A healthy veggie supper, light on the stomach and a delight to bake. The zucchinis are flavored by a mix of pine nuts, sundried tomatoes and fine parmesan cheese. You can brush the zucchinis with a bit of pesto instead of olive oil, before placing them in the oven.

Ingredients (2 servings):
2 zucchinis, halved lengthways
2 teaspoons olive oil
mixed salad, to serve

Stuffing:
25g pine nuts
3 spring onions, finely sliced
1 garlic clove, crushed
3 sundried tomatoes in oil, drained
12g parmesan, finely grated
25g dried white breadcrumbs

1 teaspoon thyme leaf

Prep time: 10 min
Cooking time: 35 min

Preparation:
Heat the oven to 200C fan/gas 7. Place the zucchinis in an
ovenproof dish, cut-side up. Brush lightly with 1 teaspoon oil
and bake for 20 min.
Mix all the stuffing ingredients together in a bowl and season
with black pepper, sprinkle the mix on top of the zucchinis and
drizzle with the remaining olive oil. Bake for another 10-15
min, until the zucchinis are softened and the topping is crisp.
Serve hot with a mixed salad.
Nutritional value per serving: 244kcal, 10g protein, 17g fat (3
saturated), 14g carbs (3g fiber, 5g sugar), 56% vitamin C, 16%
vitamin B2, 21% vitamin B6.

34. Fruit Salad

A vitamin C packed fruit salad sweetened with honey and
ready to serve in 10 min. Make this simple fruit salad sing by
adding a sprinkle of freshly-cut mint.

Ingredients (1 serving):
1 grapefruit, peel and pith cut away
2 apricots, sliced
2 oranges, peel and pith cut away
1 teaspoon clear honey

Prep time 5 min

No cooking

Preparation:
Put the apricots in a large bowl. Segment the oranges and grapefruits into the bowl to catch the juices. Stir in the honey and serve.
Nutritional value per serving: 166kcal, 4g protein, 36g carbs (8g fiber, 28g sugar), 46% vitamin A, 184% vitamin C, 13% vitamin B1.

35. Devilled Mushrooms

Treat yourself to a spicy, healthy meal, with a side of fresh, crisp salad. Double the serving for a higher fiber and protein content or pair it with a medium slice of baguette at about 150kcal per piece.

Ingredients (2 servings):
8 large flat mushrooms
2 garlic cloves, crushed
2 tablespoon olive oil
2 tablespoons Worcestershire sauce
2 tablespoons wholegrain mustard
1 teaspoon paprika
140g bag mixed salad leaves, with watercress and ruby chard

Prep time: 10 min
Cooking time: 15 min

Preparation:
Heat the oven to 180C fan/ gas 6. Mix together the mustard, oil, garlic and Worcestershire sauce in a large bowl, then

season with freshly ground black pepper and salt. Add the mushrooms to the mix and toss well to coat them evenly. Place them stalk–side up in an ovenproof dish, sprinkle them with the paprika and bake for 8-10 min.

Divide the salad leaves between two serving plates with 4 mushrooms on each plate. Spoon over the juices and serve immediately.

Nutritional value per serving: 102kcal, 8g protein, 14g fat (2g saturated), 8g carbs (4g fiber), 1g salt, 20% vitamin B2, 16% vitamin B3.

36. Smoked Trout with Beetroot, Fennel and Apple Salad

A delicate hot-smoked fish complemented by a crisp apple and the colorful beetroot, makes for an exotic salad with a gorgeous flavor combination. Trout is an ideal source of B12 and high quality protein.

Ingredients (2 servings):
140g skinless smoked trout fillet
100g baby beetroot in vinegar, drained and quartered
4 spring onions, sliced
1 green-skinned apple, cored, quartered and sliced
½ small fennel bulb, trimmed and thinly sliced
small bunch dill leaves, finely chopped
2 tablespoons low-fat yogurt
1 teaspoon horseradish sauce

Prep time: 10 min
No cooking
Preparation:

Place the fennel in a serving dish and scatter over the beetroots, spring onions and apple. Cut the trout into chunky pieces and put on top. Sprinkle with half the dill.

Mix the yogurt and horseradish with 1 tablespoon cold water, then add the rest of the dill and stir. Pour half of the dressing over the salad and toss lightly, then spoon over the rest of the dressing and serve.

Nutritional value per serving: 183kcal, 19g protein, 5g fat (1g saturated), 16g carbs (5g fiber, 16g sugar), 1.6g salt, 12% iron, 11% vitamin A, 20% vitamin C, 20% vitamin B1, 17% vitamin B2, 20% vitamin B3, 100% vitamin B12.

37. Roasted Carrots with Pomegranate and Goat Cheese

An all-round full meal when it comes to nutrients, this combination of sweet vegetables and sour juices is a healthy and interesting dinner option. Make sure to keep the pomegranate seeds separate and add them just before serving if you plan on making a big batch.

Ingredients (2 servings):
375g carrots
40g pomegranate seeds
50g goat cheese, crumbled
200g can chickpeas, drained
grated zest and juice from ½ orange
1 tablespoon olive oil
1 teaspoon cumin seeds
small bunch mint, chopped

Prep time: 10 min
Cooking time: 50 min

Preparation:
Heat the oven to 170C fan/gas 5. Put the carrots in a bowl and toss with half the olive oil, the cumin seeds and orange zest and salt. Spread the carrots onto a large baking sheet and roast for 50 min until they get tender and catch some color on the edges.

Stir the chickpeas into the roasted carrots, then tip onto a serving platter. Drizzle with the remaining oil and the orange juice. Add the crumbled goat cheese, scatter with the pomegranate seeds and herbs and serve.

Nutritional value per serving: 285kcal, 12 g protein, 15g fat (6g saturated), 30g carbs (6g fiber, 16g sugar), 15% calcium, 12% iron, 14% magnesium, 610% vitamin A, 28% vitamin C, 12% vitamin B1, 18% vitamin B2, 11% vitamin B3, 37% vitamin B6.

38. Lentil, Carrot and Orange Soup

An interesting soup made with orange juice that will more than cover your daily required amount of vitamin C. Healthy, with flavors that work well together, this recipe is a spicy delight. You can thin it with some water if you find it too thick.

Ingredients (2 servings):
75g red lentils
225g carrots, diced
300ml orange juice
1 onion, chopped
600ml vegetable stock
2 tablespoons low-fat yogurt
1 teaspoon cumin seeds
2 teaspoons coriander seeds

freshly chopped coriander to garnish

Prep time: 15min
Cooking time: 35 min

Preparation:
Crush the seeds in a pestle and mortar, then dry-fry for 2 min until lightly browned. Add the lentils, carrots, onion, orange juice, stock and seasoning and bring to a boil. Cover and simmer for 30 min until the lentils have softened.
Transfer the mix to a food processor and blend until smooth. Return to the pan, reheat at medium heat and stir occasionally. Season to taste then ladle into bowls, swirl the yogurt over, sprinkle with the coriander leaves and serve at once.
Nutritional value per serving: 184kcal, 8g protein, 2g fat, 34g carbs (4g fiber), 1g salt, 340% vitamin A, 134% vitamin C, 16% vitamin B1, 11% vitamin B3, 13% vitamin B6.

39. Veggie Red Curry

It might take almost an hour to make, but this fragrant Thai dish will surely get your taste buds into action. Rich in nutrients, this creamy veggie curry has the makings of a standalone dish, but it can be also served with a side of boiled brown rice at around 175 extra kcal.

Ingredients (2 servings):
70g mushrooms, snapped
70g sugar snap peas
½ zucchini, chopped into chunks
½ eggplant, chopped into chunks

100g firm tofu, chopped into cubes
200ml can reduced-fat coconut milk
1 red chili (½ finely chopped, ½ sliced into rounds)
¼ red pepper, deseeded and chopped into chinks
2 tablespoons soy sauce
Juice from 1 lime
1 tablespoon olive oil
10g basil leaves
½ teaspoon brown sugar

Paste:
3 shallots, roughly chopped
2 small red chilies
½ lemongrass, roughly chopped
1 garlic cloves
stalks from 10g pack coriander
½ red pepper, deseeded and roughly chopped
zest form ½ lime
¼ teaspoon grated ginger root
½ teaspoon ground coriander
½ teaspoon freshly ground pepper

Prep time: 30 min
Cooking time: 20 min.

Preparation:
Marinate the tofu in half the lime juice, 1 tablespoon soy sauce
and the chopped chili.
Place the paste ingredients in a food processor.
Heat half the oil in a pan, add 2 tablespoons of paste and fry
for 2 min. Stir in the coconut milk with 50ml water, the
eggplant, zucchini and pepper. Cook until almost tender.

Drain the tofu, pat it dry then fry it in the remaining oil in a small pan until golden.
Add the mushroom, sugar snaps and most of the basil, then season with the sugar, the rest of the lime juice and soy sauce. Cook until the mushrooms are tender, then add the tofu and heat through. Sprinkle with the basil, scatter the sliced chili and serve.
Nutritional value per serving: 233kcal, 8g protein, 18g fat (10g saturated), 11g carbs (3g fiber, 7g sugar), 3g salt, 13% calcium, 12% iron, 14% magnesium, 11% vitamin A, 65% vitamin C, 15% vitamin B1, 21% vitamin B2, 12% vitamin B3, 22% vitamin B6.

40. Mushroom Pilaf with Lemon

This low-fat mushroom pilaf is your ticket to a lighter alternative to risotto. Throw in a handful of green peas for a more colorful dish, and feel free to replace the chives with spring onions if you like.

Ingredients (2 servings):
100g brown rice
150g mushrooms, sliced
250ml vegetable stock
1 small onion, sliced
1 garlic clove, crushed
3 tablespoons light soft cheese with garlic and herbs
zest and juice from ½ lemon
small bunch of chives, snipped

Prep time: 10 min
Cooking time: 30 min

Preparation:

Place the onion in a non-stick pan, add a few tablespoons of the stock and cook for about 5 min until softened. Add the garlic and mushrooms and cook for 2 more minutes. While mixing, add the rice and lemon zest and juice. Pour in the remaining vegetable stock and seasoning and bring to a boil. Turn down the heat, cover the pan and let it simmer for 30 min until the rice is tender. Stir through half of each of the chives and soft cheese. Divide between 2 plates and serve topped with the remaining soft cheese and chives.

Nutritional value per serving : 249kcal, 12g protein, 4g fat (2g saturated), 44g carbs, 2g fiber, 4g sugar), 11% vitamin A, 23% vitamin B2.

CHAPTER 3: HOW CAN ATHLETES BENEFIT FROM MEDITATING?

Meditation can be used by athletes for different reasons: stress, anxiety, concentration, nerves, etc. Athletes can benefit from meditation by seeing a faster rate of recovery which is fundamental when trying to push yourself to the next level of performance. Training sessions will be more intense and of higher quality due to the improved level of concentration and due to the reduction of fatigue in their muscles. Most athletes will see a reduction in nervousness before and during competition which will help them compete better and more confidently.

Once you start practicing on a regular basis you will find that you have increased capacity to concentrate and focus, when it comes time to perform under pressure and under unexpected conditions. This increased capacity to focus will take you to an even higher level of performance.

Athletes with risk of heart disease can benefit significantly from meditation. Doctors are now prescribing more meditation and less medication which is common sense for some and life changing for others. By simply reducing the amount of stress an athlete is exposed to on a daily basis will reduce blood pressure levels and improve their competitiveness by being able to take on more training. Some athletes have found that meditation can often help control stress eating which is not commonly talked about but a significant factor that steers people away from reaching their peak performance. Athletes often find they are more in control of their lives after repeating meditation sessions often which reduces stress and as a direct benefit, lowers the risk of heart disease.

Weight loss is a common problem because of not having proper planning and not being able to follow diets because of lack of discipline or poor habits. MEDITATION CAN ACTUALLY HELP WITH WEIGHT LOSS TO HAPPEN when overeating is due to stress.

Athletes trying to break bad habits will find it difficult to change their old ways and start on a new path. Smoking, drinking alcohol, nervousness, getting angry, and other negative habits can be controlled through meditation as it can reduce cravings. Slowing things down and using breathing techniques to focus on overcoming bad habits when meditating can be a powerful technique that seems less obvious but more relevant when bad habits have been developed due to stress and anger.

Athletes who suffer from depression or anxiety also suffer from stress as it is a major contributor towards the first two. Negative health states can be dramatically improved through the practice of meditation on a regular basis. When you practicing meditation you will notice it easier for you to have more control over your mood and will feel more positive about the future in general. Many athletes worry too much about the outcome or past failed outcomes which are irrelevant to the present if you take the time to maximize your present potential through improved nutrition and meditation. If your goal is to control your thoughts and emotions better, you will find that meditating will calm you down and allow you not to feel overwhelmed under strenuous situations.

CHAPTER 4: THE BEST TYPES OF MEDITATION FOR SOCCER

Mindfulness

During mindfulness, athletes should be trying to stay in the present in each and every thought that they currently have entering their mind.

This type of meditation teaches you to become aware of your breathing patterns, but doesn't attempt to change them in any way through breathing practices. This is a more passive form of meditation compared to other more active forms of meditation which will require you to change your breathing patterns. Mindfulness is one of the most common types of meditation in the world and one that all athletes can greatly benefit from.

Focused meditation

Athletes using meditation are directing their thoughts to a specific problem, emotion, or object they want to focus on and find a solution for.

Begin by clearing your mind of all distractions and then taking some time to focus on just a single sound, object, or thought. You are trying to focus for as long as possible in this state of mind where you can then redirect your concentration to an objective you want to achieve.

It's your choice if you want to move on to work on any other objective or thought, or you can also just maintain that initial focus on the sound, object, or thought you first had.

Movement meditation

Movement meditation is another form of meditation you should try as well. This is a type of meditation where you focus on your breathing patterns, moving the air into and out of your lungs, while doing flowing movement patterns (with your hands) which you will repeat. You might feel uncomfortable at the beginning by moving with your eyes closed but with time you will notice it is actually very relaxing and will help you to improve your overall health.

A mind to body connection will be optimized in this type of meditation, especially for people who have trouble staying still and prefer to move around in a natural flowing motion. These movements should be slow and repetitive. The more controlled they are, the better. Doing fast, or violent movements will undo the benefit of meditating.

People who practice yoga often find this form of meditation great as it is a good compliment and similar to yoga breathing and movement exercises. Both improve control over yourself and over thoughts. For people who have never done yoga before and have already done movement meditation, will find that warming up with some yoga based exercises can often help you ease into movement meditation faster. The goal is to enter a meditative state quicker and yoga will definitely allow you to do this in a natural way. While yoga focuses more on improving flexibility and developing muscle strength, movement meditation is directed more towards a mental state and slow breathing patterns.

Mantra meditation

Mantra meditation is going to help you focus better on your thoughts and clear your mind to maximize the effect of meditating.

During mantra meditation you will be citing mantras over and over as you follow your meditative process.

A mantra could be a sound, phrase, or prayer that's chanted over and over.

We will not be focusing on spiritual meditation but it is another type of meditation besides focused meditation, mindfulness, mantra meditation, and movement meditation.

Everyone is different which means you don't have to use just one type of meditation to achieve your goals. You can use one or more forms of meditation and in different order.

CHAPTER 5: HOW TO PREPARE TO MEDITATE

Once you know what type of meditation you will be doing, you need to know how to prepare to meditate. Make sure not to rush through your meditation process as this will certainly reduce the overall effects and diminish possible results.

EQUIPMENT: Place a mat, blanket, towel, or chair where you plan to meditate.

Some people prefer to use a towel (which is great when you are traveling or out of town), or a mat to sit on or lay flat on your back on. Others prefer to sit on a chair to have a stable position that will help you not to fall asleep if you feel too relaxed.

I prefer to sit on a yoga mat as it is a position that I feel helps me focus and relax. Sometimes I warm up with yoga or static stretching so I will already have my mat ready but when I travel I simply use a thick towel.

Being comfortable is very important to get in the right state of mind so make sure you use the right equipment to get started.

TIME: Decide how long you will meditate for in advance

Make sure you decide beforehand for how long you plan on meditating and with what purpose. For something simple like focusing on being positive and breathing, you can plan on doing a short session of about 5 to 15 minutes long. Whereas if you plan on focusing on a problem and want to try and find a solution for, you might want to plan on giving yourself enough time to first relax through breathing patterns and then start to focus on alternative solutions to the problem at hand. This might take anywhere from 10 minutes to an hour or longer depending on your level of experience in meditating or it may also depend on how long it takes you to get in a relaxed state of mind that will allow you to focus well enough to confront the problem.

Plan on how long you will take so that you can prepare beforehand to stay at the same location until you're done without interruptions such as: being hungry, kids coming into the room, bathroom breaks, etc. Take care of these possible distractions beforehand.

LOCATION: Finding a clean, quiet, and comfortable space to meditate

Find a place where you can totally relax and clear your mind with no interruptions. This can be anywhere you feel comfortable and can reach this relaxed state of mind. It could be on the grass in a park, at home in your room, in your bathroom, in a quiet empty room, or by yourself in your car. This is completely up to you. Make sure you don't choose a location where you may have work close to you or a cell phone that keeps ringing or vibrating. TURN YOUR CELL PHONE OFF! It's impossible to get the results you want from meditating by having constant distractions and now a days cell phones are a main source of distraction and interruptions.

The location you choose should have these things in common: it should be quiet, clean, and needs to be at a cool room temperature (too warm will put you to sleep and too cold will make you want to get up and move around), it should be clear of distractions.

PREPARATION: Prepare your body to meditate

Before meditating make sure you do whatever you need to do to get your body relaxed and ready. This could be by taking a shower, stretching, putting on comfortable clothes, etc.

Make sure you eat at least 30 minutes before starting so that you don't feel hungry or too full. A lean meal would be ideal to help you prepare properly beforehand. I will go into more depth on the importance of nutrition in one of the following chapters.

WARM UP: Do some Yoga or stretch beforehand to start relaxing.

For some of you who have already done yoga in the past, know how relaxing it can be. Those of you who have not started doing yoga, it would be a good time to start since it will help you to better relax and calm yourself down. It's not necessary to do yoga before meditating but it helps in order to maximize the effects and speed up the relaxing process to get you in the right state of mind. Stretching is another good alternative since stretching combined with some breathing exercises will help you calm down and feel more at ease.

MENTALITY: Do some deep breathing to start calming yourself down

Breathing is easy but practicing breathing takes more time. The benefits of practicing breathing techniques are many.

Most athletes will find themselves recovering faster after intense moments. They will also notice they are able to stay focused even when out of breath. ATHLETES NEED TO LEARN TO BREATHE! Athletes need to focus on the air moving into and out of their lungs, pay attention to how the body expands and contracts. Hearing and feeling the air move in and out of your nose and mouth will help you feel more relaxed and is the proper to focus on your breathing. Every time you breathe in and is then exhaled try to focus on going into a deeper and deeper state of relaxation. Every time oxygen fills your lungs your body will feel more energized and full of positive emotions.

ENVIRONMENT: Add some meditative or relaxing music in the background only if it does not become a distraction.

If meditation music helps you get into a relaxed state, by all means include it in your meditation session. Everything and anything that helps you get into a more focused and relaxed state should be used, including music.

If you feel you are able to clear your mind better without any sounds or music, then don't add music to your environment.

I normally don't add music simply because I find music takes me in other directions which I don't always want to go since some music reminds me of other thoughts and ideas. That's just me but maybe music is right for you. Try both options to see what works better for you. Some athletes like to listen to music before competing since they feel it relaxes them or gets them in the right mood. Find what works for you and stick to it.

MEDITATING POSITIONS

When it comes to meditating positions it's basically up to you. There is no wrong or right position, only the one that gets you in the best state of concentration. For some people sitting on a chair is great because of the back support, while others prefer to be closer to the ground and will decide to sit on a towel.

For people who are less flexible the lotus position might be something you may want to skip or wait to try out as it might feel too uncomfortable to hold for a long period of time. Again, make sure you can stay in the same position for the time period you are planning to meditate for or else choose another position.

Sitting position

For the sitting position simply find a chair that you feel will allow you to focus without making you feel too uncomfortable or that relaxes you too much where you feel sleepy. Make sure your back is straight when seated and that your feet can touch the floor as you don't want to finish your meditation session with back pain. Some people prefer to add a soft pillow to their chair to feel more comfortable.

Kneeling on the floor

Take your shoes and socks off if you want to and kneel on the ground. Try kneeling on top of a soft mat or folded towel as to have your toes pointing behind you and your hips directly above your heels. Your back should be straight and relaxed as to allow your lungs to expand and contract as much times as necessary. You want to create a strong connection through your breathing and to do this, air has to go in and out of your lungs in a flowing motion.

Burmese position

The Burmese position is similar to a butterfly stretching position but with a change in the position of the feet. Sit down on the floor and open your legs, then bend your knees while bringing your feet towards the inside part of your legs. One foot should be in front of the other. When in this position try to keep your knees down as low as possible. If it feels uncomfortable choose another position as there are many options. Your hands should be at your sides or together in a finger crossing-over position. Your back should be straight and your forehead tilting slightly up and forward to allow you to take in air and release it in a full and complete manner. This is an advanced meditation position so it's not necessary to start with it unless you feel completely relaxed in it.

Lotus position

The Lotus position is very similar to the Burmese position but with a small alteration. You will need to bring your feet on top of your thighs while in a Burmese position. Your hands should be at your sides or together in a finger crossing-over position. My knees feel uncomfortable in this position so I don't use it for my meditation sessions but you are free to try it as long as it does not cause pain. You don't want the pain you feel to take all your attention from your goal of focused breathing and calmness. If you don't like this position, simply choose another.

Laying down position

Lay down on the mat, towel, or blanket and relax your feet and hands. Your hands should stay at your sides and your feet pointing up or outwards. Your hands can be placed on your stomach in a gentle but still position or at your sides. Your head needs to stay facing the ceiling or the sky. If you tilt it to one side or another, this will not allow you to stay focused for long periods of time and might even end up with some neck tension. This is a great position to meditate in (when done correctly) as long as you don't fall asleep. If this is your problem, simply choose another position.

Butterfly position
In this position you will need to sit down on your mat or towel, open your legs and then bring your feet together so that the bottom of each is facing one another. Your knees might flare upwards or they might be able to go down to the ground, it does not matter as long as you feel comfortable and can relax in this position. Make sure your spine is straight and balanced.

CHAPTER 6: MEDITATING FOR MAXIMUM SOCCER RESULTS

Meditating to reach your maximum potential will depend on your ability to focus on a thought or problem and stay focused for as long as necessary to solve the problem or until you realize your objective. This will create confidence and self-conviction for future tasks you may need to accomplish.

When you meditate and want to achieve maximum results you will need to follow these exact steps every time. If you change or eliminate any step, you will end up changing the outcome of the meditation session.

These steps are:

1st: Find a quiet place where you won't be disturbed.

2nd: Place a mat, towel, blanket, or chair where you are planning to meditate.

3rd: Make sure you had a light meal or snack about an hour before meditating.

4th: Choose a position in which you will be comfortable in for the entire session. This could be: sitting on a chair, lying down on a mat, sitting in a Burmese, Lotus or butterfly position, kneeling on a mat, or any other comfortable meditation position mentioned before.

5th: Begin your breathing pattern. If you want to calm and relax yourself you should choose to breathe more air out than you do air in (except if you are doing mindfulness meditation as you should not try to control your breathing but instead simply feel the air going into your lungs and then out into your surroundings.). For example, breathe in 4 seconds and then breathe out for 6 seconds. When trying to energize yourself because you feel too relaxed or just woke up, you would breathe more air in than out in a specific ratio which you can decide beforehand. For example, breathe 5 seconds in and 3 seconds out. Remember each sequence of breathing needs to be repeated at least 4 to 6 times to allow your breathing to slow the mind down and get you in a state of calmness to best meditate. For all breathing patterns you will breathe in through your nose and out through your mouth, except for mindfulness meditation which will be in and out through your nose only as the focus is not on your breathing.

6th: Once you are done completing your breathing patterns in the manner explained in the breathing patterns chapter, you should begin to focus on something you want to obtain, achieve, or simply preview in your mind. Focus on this for as long as possible. Short sessions give you shorter lasting results while longer sessions tend to help you maintain this level of concentration even after you're done meditating. All athletes know that when it's time to perform, (especially when under pressure), they need to stay focused and being able to do this for a longer period of time without losing concentration will permit them to outperform the competition. **This is the difference between champions and the rest!**

7th: This thought should now evolve to a short or long mental movie clip you are creating in your mind to help you achieve what you want in your mind first, with the goal to eventually make it happen in a real life situation. Be as specific as possible and stay relaxed in the process. This seventh step adds visualizing to the process but there's nothing wrong with that as it can only benefit you but it's necessary if you just want to keep it simple.

8th: Athletes need to use breathing to finish their meditation sessions to end as they began. If you don't have to compete on the same day, you can use slow breathing patterns such as the example below:

Normal slow breathing pattern: Start by taking air in through your nose slowly and counting to 5. Then, release slowly counting back down from 5 to 1. You should repeat this process 4 to 10 times until you feel completely relaxed and ready to meditate. Athletes should focus on breathing in through the nose and out through the mouth for this type of breathing pattern.

If you have to compete the same day you should energize your mind and body at the end by using fast breathing patterns such as the one below:

Normal fast breathing pattern: Start by taking air in through your nose slowly and counting to 5. Then, release slowly counting back down from 3 to 1. You should repeat this process 6 to 10 times until you feel completely relaxed but energized. Athletes should focus on breathing in through the nose and out through the mouth for this type of breathing pattern.

CHAPTER 7: VISUALIZATION TECHNIQUES FOR IMPROVED SOCCER RESULTS

The three main types of visualization techniques:

There are many types of visualizations that can be performed. Three common types are motivational visualizations, problem solving visualizations, and goal oriented visualizations.

Athletes in all fields commonly use visualizations in one form or another sometimes without even knowing they are doing them. For some, it's done while being awake which is what is known as day dreaming and for others this might happen in their dreams but with no control over the outcome.

When you are visualizing you are in control of everything you're seeing in your mind and can design the beginning and ending however you like. Being creative is useful since things don't always come out the way we plan them to in real life but by preparing mentally and emotionally for all possible outcomes, things become easier to handle when it comes time to perform. Peak performance is a term used for when you are "in the zone" and at your very best. It is easier to perform at your peak when you have prepared your mind through visualizations.

Why visualize to motivate yourself?

Some people have trouble finding the right motivation under pressure to do what they are supposed to be doing instead of being intimidated by their surroundings and people watching them. By motivating yourself through visualizations and by telling yourself to do better and push yourself harder as you see the thoughts you want to realize in your mind, you will unlock the brains possibilities to get you through the fear, anxiety, nervousness, and pressure involved when competing.

What are problem solving visualizations?
Problem solving visualizations are a common form of mental training and can be the most useful of all visualization techniques. Often, athletes find they keep making the same mistakes over and over only to find the same result. This is because they need to take the time to analyze the situation and search for all possible solutions to their problems. Simply finding time to visualize will be time well spent when you need to solve a specific problem. Having too many distractions during the day, both mental and visual, can slow down the speed at which you could find a solution to what you would like to correct. It could be a habit you have formed that you can't get rid of. It can also be that you do your worst right when it counts the most. Other times it can be that you lose your temper or get too emotional right when you need to keep your cool.

There are many possible situations an athlete can be in and not know how to approach them is the main reason success is delayed or never realized.

The first step is to find the time to problem solve and visualize.

The second step to problem solving is to determine what the problem is and how it's affecting you.

The third step is to find alternative solutions that can take you in the right direction or that can eliminate the problem. In some cases, you might have to ask others who have been in similar situations and find out how they approached this problem and if their solution is an option for you.

The fourth step is to visualize how you would physically perform this solution and make it as vivid and real as you can.

The fifth step is to make corrections when you have mentally seen that it won't work and find an alternative. You can also simply apply the solution in real life and if it does not work go back to visualizing later to find a better solution. This is more of a "trial and error" method than visualization technique but can be used as a practical tool to get you there by combining it with visualizations.

What are goal oriented visualizations?

Goal oriented visualizations are mental images and videos you want to create in your brain when visualizing that focus on achieving a specific objective. This may be: winning a competition, improving your record time, training more hours a day, adding "X" amount of protein to your diet, not getting tired as much (some of these are results based goals and some are performance based goals. Both are important when planning your visualization session and future progress as an athlete.)

This is what you train physically for. To see results at the end of all the hard work. Using visualizations completes the training by doing the last and most important part of preparing for competition. You prepare your mind and body to perform at their best so that you can do it when it counts the most. Nutrition and physical training will prepare your body. Meditation, breathing patterns, and visualizations will prepare your brain. The combination of both will give you the greatest competitive advantage and that's you want.

CHAPTER 8: VISUALIZATION TECHNIQUES: MOTIVATIONAL VISUALIZATIONS

Learning to get inspired

Getting inspired by seeing yourself be successful through visualizations is a great image to experience and a wonderful effect visualizing can create in your life. Learn to get inspired and believe things are possible in your own life because they are. Athletes often limit themselves because they don't dream big enough. With a little planning and some discipline many things are possible no matter how difficult they may seem.

What are motivational visualizations?

Motivational visualizations are mental images you will create where you see yourself being confident, radiant, and successful. Inspiring yourself through an amplified positive self-image is powerful and can have ripple effects in other parts of your life.

You should be imagining yourself reach a goal when visualizing. These are some questions you want to ask yourself when preparing to perform motivational visualizations:

- How would you like to dress to compete if you could choose any uniform, clothes, or attire?
- How would you walk before competing if you had all the confidence in the world?
- What would be the perfect environment for you to compete in?
- What facial expressions would you have if you were to win?

- How would you look if you lost 10 pounds of fat and were leaner, faster, and more explosive?
- How would you look if you felt confident?
- What would you do if you won the competition or reached your goal?

By seeing yourself being successful with a goal you are trying to build up the desire to reach it so that you give as much effort as possible to get there. Having a strong will to reach your objectives will boost your chances to break through and realize mental victory which will make real victory possible. Motivational visualizations can be used for different purposes in your personal life, which can improve your overall performance in your athletic life as well especially if you are trying to give up a vice like smoking, alcohol, uncontrollable anger or fear, over eating, partying, gambling, etc.

CHAPTER 9: VISUALIZATION TECHNIQUES: PROBLEM SOLVING VISUALIZATIONS

Visualizations should be done properly and directed towards the best problem solving techniques. For this reason determining what will work best is the most important step. For this reason we are going to look at how most athletes approach their problems.

How do most athletes approach problem solving?

There are many ways athletes approach their problems and attempt to solve them. "Attempt" is the key word.

These are the most often seen examples of how athletes approach problem solving:

The anger solution

They get mad at their problems and get frustrated to the point where their brain helps little or nothing because they're so overcome by their negative emotions.

Anger is an emotional reaction that is normal and common but not necessarily a solution that will bring about positive results. When attempting to solve your problems, emotions need to be set aside so that you can better concentrate on the real problem that needs to be addressed.

Managing anger is difficult for some and can take time to overcome but specific activities such as visualizations, meditation, and yoga are a great way to start.

The "blame-game" solution

Athletes who blame others for their mistakes or problems knowingly make an effort not to blame themselves. Blaming others for your errors or problems is the easy way out of justifying lack of success but does not solve the problem at all. Others blame their equipment and/or surroundings without considering that changes in climate and surroundings will affect all competitors and not just them. Blaming equipment failure is simply not what should be focused on since proper preparation can easily solve this problem. Sometimes the equipment might not have any flaws at all and is just a way of blaming something other than themselves. Taking responsibility for their actions is the hardest but the most productive way to advance to a real solution.

The "whining" solution

Whining and complaining makes your voice be heard by others and yourself but only delays the inevitable result of failure since steps are not being taken to remedy the situation. Whining starts at a young age when you don't get what you want but the worst thing that can happen is being given that which you're complaining for because it does not allow you to solve the problem correctly.

Learning to cope with a negative performance should be a key element when developing mental toughness. Becoming mentally tough does not happen because you have had an easy path to success. Its normally comes from not giving in to negative results and failure.

The "stop-trying" solution

Not making any effort to succeed and basically giving up is a choice some athletes make but it's not one to be proud of since so many better options exist. Training your brain to find alternatives to succeed instead of giving up will always be a better path and a more fruitful one.

The "repeat-offender" solution

The repeat-offender is the athlete that keeps making the same mistake over and over expecting a different result. We have all been victims of this mental error but it can become a turning point for those of you who acknowledge this fault and want to make a true change in your results.

Simply changing how you solve your problem is already an improvement even though it's not a precise direction which you're following but it's a different path and a different path will give you a chance to change things.

The "trial and error" solution

The "trial and error" solution is simply trying new approaches to your problem and seeing if they are a solution to the problem. The outcome will be that you will eventually find the right solution to your problem but it might take you long than you would like or longer than you can afford.

This is a much better approach than the last mentioned solutions but you can learn to make even better choices by separating certain factors and conditions from your options and that's what we will see next.

The "best probability" solution

When solving problems, we all know that we have alternatives and choices we can make to find a solution but knowing which one of them will be more useful and worth visualizing on is what matters the most.

Using probabilities helps you quantify that which you are trying to solve in your mind.

For example, if you find that every time you warm up you start to get nervous but don't know why. Eventually, once you complete your warm up nerves go away and you feel fine. Now you know that focusing on visualizing on your actual performance would only account for less than 10% of the problem since you know that the warm up is really 90% of your problem. You can work on your performance mentally but finding a solving to your warm up problem will provide you with the most valuable results since it accounts for 90% of your problem and will result in a 90% improvement in your overall performance.

Another example would be if you find that every time you are in a pressure situation you freeze and underperform. That key moment accounts for 100% of your results based on past performances. Since it will represent the most change in what you want to achieve you should focus 100% of your visualization sessions on finding solutions to that key moment. That way you will be most productive with your time. Focusing on what matters the most will make the biggest change so learn to concentrate and direct your visualizations on what will help you the most and not on unimportant problems that even if solved won't create a true improvement in your results.

CHAPTER 10: VISUALIZATION TECHNIQUES: GOAL ORIENTED VISUALIZATIONS

Performance based goals vs results based goals

Before starting any goal oriented visualizations you should have a clear image of what you want to gain from visualizing and what the best path will be to get there.

What are performance based goals?

Performance based goals are simple goals that can be reached by doing things you know you need to do to be successful. These can be physical or mental. Not looking at the competition or family and friends while performing is a great example of a performance based goal you can have for yourself. If are able to reach that goal after competing then you have accomplished what you set out to do and will be much closer to reaching your results based goals.

Another example of a performance based goal is to focus on staying calm and breathe during competition. Reaching this goal at the end will be your objective. Achieving this goal will help you get much closer to being successful and realizing your potential. It's a simple and easy to obtain goal that you have 100% control over. If you don't make it the first time, you know that if you keep trying you will eventually get there and can then create a new harder or different performance based goal.

These are other examples of performance goals that athletes can have:
- Do 1 more push-up every day.
- Stretch for 10 minutes a day.

- Breathe in and out under pressure.
- Focus your eyes on the task at hand and not on your surroundings.
- Stay calm when underperforming.
- Stay energized when you feel yourself freezing under difficult situations.

You can create your own performance based goals and make them harder want as long as their attainable.

What are results based goals?
Results based goals are goals you make for yourself which are focused on end results and not the process to get there. Some examples of a results based goal is to win, to reach the final of a competition, to lift "x" weight, to have the best time, to finish first, etc. Athletes can have different goals and still reach the same objective.

Some examples of results based goals that athletes can have are:
- Win 5 championships before the end of the year.
- Break a world record.
- Finish first in your country.
- Win your first medal or trophy.
- Help your team get to their first final.
- Jump higher than you have ever before.
- Run your fastest time.
- Swim the furthest you ever have.
- Reach the finish line before everyone else.

Results based goals are the result of consistent, organized, and gradually increasing performance goals.

When visualizing you need to visualize success in both reaching your performance and results based goals. You can alternate days to focus on one and then the other or simply stick to performance based goals first and once you feel that you are comfortably reaching them, you can move on to results based goals.

Having goals is the key to moving forward and should be visualized on at least once a week so that you have a clear image of what you are working on to reach. It's the best way to move forward and see yourself advance through the process. Without goals you won't have a path to follow towards success. Map out that path in your mind through your visualizations and then turn them into reality by putting them into practice when training or competing.

CHAPTER 11: BREATHING TECHNIQUES TO MAXIMIZE YOUR VISUALIZATION EXPERIENCE AND ENHANCE YOUR PERFORMANCE

Breathing patterns will be the key to set the pace of your visualization session and also to get into a hyper focused state. When visualizing, you want to pay attention to breathing patterns and direct them through your session. All breathing patterns should be done by breathing in through your nose and out through your mouth.

In order to get into a more relaxed state, your heart rate needs to drop and to do this, breathing will be essential. The patterns you use will facilitate this process to help you reach higher levels of concentration. With practice these breathing patterns will become second nature to you. Decide beforehand if slow breathing patterns are better for you or if fast breathing patterns will be what you need. Slow breathing patterns relax you and fast breathing patterns energize you.

SLOW BREATHING PATTERNS

In order to slow down your breathing you will want to take in air slowly and for a longer period of time and then release it slowly as well. For athletes, this type of breathing is good to get you to relax after training or about an hour before competition. Different ratios of air in and air out will affect your level of relaxation, and in turn your ability to reach an optimal level of visualization.

Normal slow breathing pattern: Start by taking air in through your nose slowly and counting to 5. Then, release slowly counting back down from 5 to 1. You should repeat this process 4 to 10 times until you feel completely relaxed and ready to focus. Athletes should focus on breathing in through the nose and out through the mouth for this type of breathing pattern.

Extended slow breathing pattern: Start by taking air in through your nose slowly and counting to 7. Then, release slowly counting back down from 7 to 1 while exhaling out through your mouth. You should repeat this process 4 to 6 times until you feel completely relaxed and ready to focus.

Slow breathing pattern for hyperactive athletes: Start by taking air in through your nose slowly and counting to 3. Then, release slowly counting back down from 6 to 1 while exhaling out through your mouth. You should repeat this process 4 to 6 times until you feel relaxed and ready to focus. This pattern will force you to slow down completely. The last repetition of this sequence should end with 4 seconds in and 4 seconds out to stabilize your breathing.

Ultra slow breathing pattern: Begin by taking air in through your nose slowly and counting to 4. Then, release slowly counting back down from 10 to 1 while exhaling out through your mouth. You should repeat this process 4 to 6 times until you feel completely relaxed and ready to visualize. This pattern will force you to slow down gradually. The last 2 repetitions of this sequence should end with 4 seconds in and 4 seconds out to stabilize your breathing and balance the air in and out ratio.

Stabilizing breathing patterns before meditating: This is a good type of breathing pattern that should be used if you feel you are already calm and want to start immediately meditating. Start by taking air in through your nose slowly and counting to 3. Then, release slowly counting back down from 3 to 1. You should repeat this process 7 to 10 times until you feel completely relaxed and ready to focus. Athletes should focus on breathing in through the nose and out through the mouth for this type of breathing pattern.

FAST BREATHING PATTERNS

Fast breathing patterns are very important for athletes in order to get energized and ready to compete. Even though this type of breathing pattern is most effective when visualizing, it will be just as useful for meditating. For athletes that are very calm and need to feel more in control of their mind might want to use these patterns to get themselves ready to visualize.

Normal fast breathing pattern: Start by taking air in through your nose slowly and counting to 5. Then, release slowly counting back down from 3 to 1. You should repeat this process 6 to 10 times until you feel completely relaxed and ready to visualize. Athletes should focus on breathing in through the nose and out through the mouth for this type of breathing pattern.

Prolonged fast breathing pattern: Start by taking air in through your nose slowly and counting to 10. Then, release slowly counting back down from 5 to 1 while exhaling out through your mouth. You should repeat this process 5 to 6 times until you feel completely relaxed. If you have trouble getting to 10 at first, simply lower the count to 7 or 8. Focus on breathing in through the nose and out through the mouth.

Pre-competition fast breathing pattern: Start by taking air in through your nose slowly and counting to 6. Then, release quickly in one breath while exhaling out through your mouth.

You should repeat this process 5 to 6 times until you feel completely relaxed and ready to focus. You can add 2 repetitions to this sequence with 4 seconds in and 4 seconds out to stabilize your breathing and balance the air in and out ratio.

All of these types of breathing patterns are performance enhancing and can be used during competition depending on your level of energy or nervousness.

For athletes that get nervous before competition you should use slow breathing patterns.

For athletes that need to get energized before competition you should use the fast breathing patterns.

In case of anxiety, a combination of slow breathing patterns followed by fast breathing patterns will give you optimal results.

During training sessions or during competition when feeling exhausted or out of breath use the normal fast breath breathing pattern to help recover quicker.

Breathing patterns are a great way to control your levels of intensity which in turn will save you energy and allow you to recover faster.

CLOSING COMMENTS

Having an organized training, nutrition, and mental toughness plan can make all the difference in the world. Taking the time to work and develop each aspect of this book will give you the best results and will allow your body to adapt to this new and better form of preparation. Not knowing what to do or how to start making a change for good is the most common reason most people don't improve their performance after a certain point. This book will guide you through the most important parts of a complete training program and allow you to reach a new "ULTIMATE" you.

OTHER GREAT TITLES BY THIS AUTHOR

THE BEST MUSCLE BUILDING SHAKE RECIPES FOR

SOCCER

HIGH PROTEIN SHAKES TO MAKE YOU STRONGER AND FASTER

By
JOSEPH CORREA
Certified Sports Nutritionist

Made in the USA
Lexington, KY
01 July 2016